First World War
and Army of Occupation
War Diary
France, Belgium and Germany

62 DIVISION
Divisional Troops
Royal Army Medical Corps
2/1 West Riding Field Ambulance
12 January 1917 - 29 August 1919

WO95/3078/1

The Naval & Military Press Ltd
www.nmarchive.com
Published in association with The National Archives

Published by

The Naval & Military Press Ltd

Unit 10 Ridgewood Industrial Park,

Uckfield, East Sussex,

TN22 5QE England

Tel: +44 (0) 1825 749494

www.naval-military-press.com

www.nmarchive.com

This diary has been reprinted in facsimile from the original. Any imperfections are inevitably reproduced and the quality may fall short of modern type and cartographic standards.

© **Crown Copyright**
Images reproduced by permission of The National Archives, London, England, 2015.

Contents

Document type	Place/Title	Date From	Date To
Heading	WO95/3078/1 2/1 West Riding Field Ambulance		
Heading	62nd Division 2-1st (W.R.) Fld Ambulance Jan 1917-1919 Aug		
Heading	War Diary of Lt Col W. Lister R.A.M.C.T Commdg 21st W.R Fd Ambulance From 8th July 1917 To 30th July 1917 (Volume 1.)		
War Diary	Boffles	12/01/1917	21/01/1917
War Diary	Map Ref 57d.I.10.c 66	22/01/1917	30/02/1917
Heading	2nd Division 2/1st W.R. Field Ambulance		
Heading	War Diary of 2/1st W.R. Field Ambulance From 1.2.17 To 28.2.17 Vol 2		
War Diary	Bois Laleau	01/02/1917	13/02/1917
War Diary	Bethancourt	14/02/1917	21/02/1917
War Diary	Mailly Maillet	22/02/1917	27/02/1917
War Diary	62nd Div. 2/1st W.R. Field Ambulance		
Heading	War Diary of 2/1st West Riding Field Ambulance From 1st March/17 To 31st March/17 (Volume III)		
War Diary	Mailly-Maillet Q18c.2.1	01/03/1917	01/03/1917
War Diary	Q 18 C 21	02/03/1917	31/03/1917
Heading	62nd Div. 2/1st West Riding F.A		
Heading	War Diary of 2/2nd W.R. Field Ambulance Royal Army Medical Corps (T.F.) From 1st Apl/1917 To 30th Apl/1917 Volume IV		
War Diary	Q18 C21	01/04/1917	01/04/1917
War Diary	Lancashire Dump	02/04/1917	04/04/1917
War Diary	Q35 D.28	05/04/1917	13/04/1917
War Diary	G.9 B.6.3	14/04/1917	24/04/1917
War Diary	H1 D97	25/04/1917	28/04/1917
Heading	62nd Div. 2/1st, West Riding F.A.		
Heading	War Diary Of 2/1st West Riding F. Ambce From May 1st 1917 To May 31st 1917 Volume 5.		
War Diary	H.1.D.97	01/05/1917	13/05/1917
War Diary	Courcelles	14/05/1917	29/05/1917
War Diary	G9.A.10.8	30/05/1917	31/05/1917
Heading	2/1st West Riding F.A. June 1917		
Heading	War Diary of 2/1st West Riding Field Ambulance From 1st June To June 30th 1917 Vol. 6		
War Diary	Map 57c.G9.b2.7.	01/06/1917	24/06/1917
War Diary	G.9.b.2.7	25/06/1917	25/06/1917
War Diary	H.16.d.7.5.	26/06/1917	30/06/1917
Heading	2/1st West Riding F.A. July 1917		
Heading	War Diary Of Lieut. Colonel Walter Lister RAMC (T) Commdg 2/1st West Riding Field Ambce. for The Month of July 1917		
War Diary	Map.57c H.16.d.7.5	01/07/1917	31/07/1917
Heading	2/1st West Riding F.A. Aug 1917		
Heading	War Diary Of 2/1st W.R. Field Ambulance Period 1st To 31st Aug17 Volume VIII		
War Diary	In The Field H16.D.7.5. Map 57c	01/08/1917	31/08/1917

Heading	War Diary of 2/1st West Riding Field Ambce From 1st Sept 1917 To 30th Sept 1917 Volume IX		
War Diary	In The Field	01/09/1917	30/09/1917
War Diary	War Diary of 2/1st West Riding Field Ambulance From 1-10-17 To 31-10-17 Volume X		
War Diary	In The Field	01/10/1917	31/10/1917
Heading	War Diary Of 2/1st West Riding Field Ambce Period-Nov 1st To Nov 30th Volume XI		
War Diary	In The Field	01/11/1917	30/11/1917
Heading	2/1st West Riding F.A.Dec 1917		
Heading	War Diary Of 2/1st West Riding Field Ambulance Period 1st-31st Decr/17 Volume XII		
War Diary	In The Field	01/12/1917	31/12/1917
Heading	War Diary Of 2/1st West Riding Field Ambce Period Jany 1st/18 To Jany 31st/18 Volume XIII		
War Diary	In The Field	01/01/1918	31/01/1918
Miscellaneous	Plans of the D.S at St Catherine detached field with Plans		
Heading	War Diary Of 2/1st West Riding Field Ambce Period 1st To 28th February 1918 Volume XIV		
War Diary	St Catherine Sheet 57b G.15.a.2.5	01/02/1918	09/02/1918
War Diary	Hermin Sheet 36b P28 A.7.8	10/02/1918	27/02/1918
War Diary	Moul St Eloi Sheet 51c.7.8 C.9.5	28/02/1918	28/02/1918
Map	Map		
Heading	War Diary Of 2/1st West Riding Fld Ambce Period 1st March 18 To 31st March 18 Volume XIV		
War Diary	Mont-St-Eloi 51c F8.D3.3.	01/03/1918	03/03/1918
War Diary	Aubigny 51c C.R.S E.1 C.5.4 O.R.S D.12.b.5.8	05/03/1918	24/03/1918
War Diary	Arras	25/03/1918	25/03/1918
War Diary	Bienvillers	26/03/1918	26/03/1918
War Diary	Humbercamps	26/03/1918	27/03/1918
War Diary	La Cauchie 51c V.17b 7.2.	27/03/1918	31/03/1918
Diagram etc	Diagram		
Diagram etc	Chart Showing no of Cases Scabies remaining in C.R.S at 2pm & 6 pm daily		
Heading	War Diary Of 2/1st West Riding Field Ambce R.A.M.C. (T) Period April 1st To 30th Inclusive Volume XVI		
War Diary	Sheet 51c V17 B7.2. LA Cauchie	01/04/1918	02/04/1918
War Diary	Sheet 57d.d.19.a.6.9. Henu	03/04/1918	06/04/1918
War Diary	Souastre Sheet 57d D22 D.6.5	07/04/1918	15/04/1918
War Diary	Pas Sheet 57d C.22 A.7.8	17/04/1918	24/04/1918
War Diary	Marieux Sheet 57d. H30.d.5.9	25/04/1918	29/04/1918
Heading	War Diary Of 2/1st West Riding Field Ambce R.A.M.C. (T) Period 1st To 31st May Inclusive Volume XVII		
War Diary	Sheet 57d Marieux H30.a.5.9	01/05/1918	13/05/1918
War Diary	Sheet 57d. Marieux Wood I.9 C.2.2	14/05/1918	16/05/1918
War Diary	Souastre Sheet 57d D.22.a.7.2	17/05/1918	17/05/1918
War Diary	Waggon Lincs Sheet 57D-D.13.d.4.4	17/05/1918	29/05/1918
War Diary	Souastre	30/05/1918	30/05/1918
Diagram etc	M.D.S Souastre		
Heading	War Diary Of 2/1st West Riding Field Ambce Period 1st To 30th June 1918 Volume XVIII		
War Diary	57D.D.22.a.7.2 M.D.S Souastre	01/06/1918	03/06/1918
War Diary	Sheet 57 D D.22.a.4.6	04/06/1918	20/06/1918

War Diary	Soustre	22/06/1918	24/06/1918
War Diary	Thievres Sheet 57 D I.1.d.2.4	25/06/1918	28/06/1918
Diagram etc	Temporary M.D.S		
Heading	War Diary Of 2/1st West Riding Field Ambce R.A.M.C. (T) Period 1st 31st July 1918 Volume XIX		
War Diary	Thievres 57 D.I.1.d.0.4	01/07/1918	01/07/1918
War Diary	C.R.S. Authie 57 D.i.15.b.2.9	02/07/1918	15/07/1918
War Diary	In Train	15/07/1918	16/07/1918
War Diary	Soudron	17/07/1918	17/07/1918
War Diary	Bisseuil	18/07/1918	18/07/1918
War Diary	St Imoges	19/07/1918	31/07/1918
Diagram etc	62nd Div. M.D.S St Imoges		
Miscellaneous	Operation Order By Lieut. Col Walter Lister Commanding 2/1st West Riding Field Amb	14/07/1918	14/07/1918
Heading	War Diary Of 2/1 West Riding Field Ambulance Period 1st To 31st Aug 1918 Volume XIX		
War Diary	Map Sheet Chalons No50 St Imoges	01/08/1918	06/08/1918
War Diary	Adq Vauchelles map 57 D I.34.b.1.1	07/08/1918	18/08/1918
War Diary	Louvencourt 57d I.34.8.1.1	19/08/1918	19/08/1918
War Diary	Pommers 57 D B.6.c.8.1	20/08/1918	20/08/1918
War Diary	Sheet 57C5.17.b.1	20/08/1918	21/08/1918
War Diary	Sheet 57 D F.11.c.4.9	23/08/1918	24/08/1918
War Diary	Ayette	24/08/1918	24/08/1918
War Diary	Courcelles A.16.d.8.5 Map Sheet 57c.N.W.	25/08/1918	31/08/1918
Miscellaneous	Report No 1	26/08/1918	26/08/1918
Miscellaneous	Report No.3	26/08/1918	26/08/1918
Miscellaneous	Report No.5	28/08/1918	28/08/1918
Miscellaneous	Report No.7	29/08/1918	29/08/1918
Heading	War Diary Of 2/1st West Riding Field Ambulance Period 1st 30th Sept 1918 Volume 21		
War Diary	Mapsheet 57 D.f.11.c.4.9 Ayette	01/09/1918	01/09/1918
War Diary	Behagnies H.1.b.6.7 (Waterlot Farm)	02/09/1918	27/09/1918
Diagram etc	62 Divisional Best Station 2/1st W.r Field Ambce		
Miscellaneous			
Heading	War Diary Of 2/1st West Riding Field Ambulance Period 1st To 30th Oct 1918 Volume XXII		
War Diary	Behagnies Sheet 57 C Waterlot Farm H1.2.6.7	01/10/1918	04/10/1918
War Diary	Beaumetz Les Cambrai J.13.b.4.2. Sheet 57c	06/10/1918	09/10/1918
War Diary	Havrincourt K33.b.6.5 Sheet 57c	10/10/1918	10/10/1918
War Diary	Marcoing L.22.b.05 Sheet 57c	11/10/1918	11/10/1918
War Diary	Cattenieres H.12.a.7.2 Sheet 57 B.	12/10/1918	13/10/1918
War Diary	Bevillers C29.a.2.8 Sheet 57 B	14/10/1918	31/10/1918
Heading	War Diary Of 2/1st West Riding Field Ambce Period 1st To 30th Nov/18 Volume XXIII		
War Diary	Solesmes	01/11/1918	03/11/1918
War Diary	Romeries	04/11/1918	05/11/1918
War Diary	Escarmain	06/11/1918	06/11/1918
War Diary	Orsinval	07/11/1918	07/11/1918
War Diary	Gommegnies	09/11/1918	12/11/1918
War Diary	Sous Le Bois	15/11/1918	16/11/1918
War Diary	Ferriere Le Grd	18/11/1918	18/11/1918
War Diary	Montignies	19/11/1918	19/11/1918
War Diary	Marbaix	20/11/1918	20/11/1918
War Diary	Fromiee	21/11/1918	21/11/1918
War Diary	Mettet	25/11/1918	25/11/1918
War Diary	Warnant	26/11/1918	26/11/1918

War Diary	Senenne	27/11/1918	27/11/1918
War Diary	Chapois	28/11/1918	28/11/1918
Heading	War Diary Of 2/1st West Riding Field Ambulance Period 1/31 Dec.1918 Volume XXIV		
War Diary	Chapois Scy	06/12/1918	10/12/1918
War Diary	Chardeneux	11/12/1918	11/12/1918
War Diary	Hamoir	12/12/1918	12/12/1918
War Diary	Habiemont	13/12/1918	13/12/1918
War Diary	Gd Halleux	14/12/1918	14/12/1918
War Diary	Renscheux	15/12/1918	16/12/1918
War Diary	Amel	17/12/1918	17/12/1918
War Diary	Berg	20/12/1918	21/12/1918
War Diary	Remscheid	22/12/1918	22/12/1918
War Diary	Hellenthal	23/12/1918	23/12/1918
War Diary	Strempt	24/12/1918	24/12/1918
War Diary	Gehn	29/12/1918	31/12/1918
Heading	War Diary Of 2/1st West Riding Field Ambce Period 1st Jany 1919 To 31st Jany 19 Volume XXV		
War Diary	Glehn	01/01/1919	31/01/1919
Heading	War Diary of 2/1st West Riding Field Ambulance From 1st Feb 1919 To 28th Feb 1919 Volume XXV		
War Diary	Glehn	01/02/1919	26/02/1919
Heading	War Diary of 2/1st West Riding Field Ambulance From 1st March 1919 To 31st March 1919 Volume XXXI		
War Diary	Glehn	01/03/1919	13/03/1919
War Diary	Wollersheim	14/03/1919	31/03/1919
Heading	War Diary Of 2/1st West Riding Field Ambulance R.A.M.C. T. Period 1st To 30th April 1919 Volume XXXVII		
War Diary	Wollersheim	04/04/1919	30/04/1919
Heading	War Diary of 2/1st West Riding Field Ambulance From 1st May 1919 To 31st May 1919 Volume XXVIII		
War Diary	Wollersheim	02/05/1919	09/05/1919
War Diary	Heimbach	10/05/1919	29/05/1919
Heading	War Diary of 2/1st (W.R.) Field Amb From 1st July 1919 To 31st July 1919 War Diary of 2/1st West Riding Field Amb From 1st July 19191 To 31st July 1919 Volume XXXI		
War Diary	Duren	01/07/1919	01/07/1919
War Diary	Heimbach	02/07/1919	19/07/1919
War Diary	Heinbach	22/07/1919	31/07/1919
Heading	War Diary of 2/1st West Riding Field Ambulance From 1st Aug 19191 To 31st Aug 19191 Volume XXXII		
War Diary	Heimbach Army Of Rhine	08/08/1919	08/08/1919
War Diary	Duren	09/08/1919	10/08/1919
War Diary	Calais	11/08/1919	11/08/1919
War Diary	England	11/08/1919	12/08/1919
War Diary	Catterick Camp	12/08/1919	29/08/1919

WO95/3078/1
2/1 West Riding Field Ambulance

62ND DIVISION

2-1ST (W.R.) FLD AMBULANCE

JAN. 1917 - ~~DEC 1918~~
            " 1919 AUG

ORIGINAL

2nd Div.

140/194/1 Vol 1

WAR DIARY
or
INTELLIGENCE SUMMARY
(Erase heading not required.)

Army Form C. 2118

Confidential
War Diary
of
West Riding R.A.M.C. Nominally 2/1st W.R. Fd AMBULANCE.
from 8th Jany 1917 to 30th Jany 1917.
(Volume I.)

COMMITTEE FOR THE
MEDICAL HISTORY OF THE WAR
Date 13 MAR. 1917

Secret and
Confidential Original

ORIGINAL

Army Form C. 2118.

WAR DIARY
or
INTELLIGENCE=SUMMARY.
(Erase heading not required.)

2/1st W.R. FIELD AMBULANCE
ROYAL ARMY MEDICAL CORPS (T.F.)

Instructions regarding War Diaries and Intelligence
Summaries are contained in F. S. Regs., Part II.
and the Staff Manual respectively. Title pages
will be prepared in manuscript.

Place	Date	Hour	Summary of Events and Information	Remarks and references to Appendices
Boulogne	12/3/17		Unit left Bedford 4-30 am January 8th. Arrived at Southampton early forenoon same day. Embarked at 4-5 pm. Boat left Port at 7-0 pm. Weather fine, good sea rough. Arrived off Havre about 5-0 am. Sea very rough. Bates and anchor lost. After four hour attempt to boat proceeded in making Harbour. Horses & mules were considerably knocked about. One of our horses down and trampled on. It died after landing. Replaced from remount at Havre. After disembarkation completed about 9-0 pm proceeded to No. 2 Rest Camp about 5 miles from boat. Reported to camp commandant. Nurses picked out. Personnel under canvas. Received instructions from Camp Commandant to proceed to point of entrainment. Moved out of Camp at 10.45 pm. Arrived at point of entrainment at 12.30 and reported to R.T.O. Entrained Ladies & wagons & personnel. Train left at 3-0 am. Proceeded to Pont Remy en route to	

T2134. Wt. W708-776. 500000. 4/15. Sir J.C. & S.

Secret & confidential

Army Form C. 2118.

2/1st W.R. F'd. Ambulance
ROYAL ARMY MEDICAL CORPS (T.F.)

WAR DIARY
or
INTELLIGENCE—SUMMARY.
(Erase heading not required.)

Place	Date	Hour	Summary of Events and Information	Remarks and references to Appendices
Boffles	12/2/17		Abbeville. Delayed in sidings at Pont Remy Informed by Station Master that we were to proceed to Prevent. Arrived Prevent at 9-0 pm. On the 11th Disentrained Instructed by Staff Captain, 185th Brigade (Capt Floyd) to proceed to Boffles. Weather cold, snowstorm and wind. Arrived at Boffles 12-0 midnight Billets allotted by Interpreter attached to 2/5 W. Yorks Reg. Wagons parked and horses under shelter. Billets very dilapidated	
	12/2/17		Billets rearranged and men made more comfortable. Water supply - well. Water obtained from fatigue by Mayor of Boffles useful.	
do	13/2/17		Difficulty experienced in obtaining fuel. No other coal. Keen frost. Personnel other than fatigues went short route marches.	
	14/2/17		Proceeded A.D.M.S. Interviewed D.A.D.M.S. and received instructions to open Detention Hospital	

Army Form C. 2118.

2/3rd W.R. FIELD AMBULANCE
ROYAL ARMY MEDICAL CORPS (T.F.)

WAR DIARY
or
INTELLIGENCE SUMMARY
(Erase heading not required.)

Place	Date	Hour	Summary of Events and Information	Remarks and references to Appendices
Béthune	15/1/17		Met assistance of Mayor obtained a house for hospital accommodation. C Section put in charge. 81 cases were admitted up to Jan 21st. Evacuation to prevent.	R
do	16/1/17		Weather cold. Short route marches and gas helmet drill. 1 Sergeant 7 Drivers and 1 dispatch Rider A.S.C. with 5 Daimler and 2 Ford Ambulances and 1 Douglas motor cycle reported for duty.	R
do	17/1/17		Training	R
do	18/1/17		Training.	R
do	19/1/17		6 Corporals were reduced it to the ranks and 2 to L/Cpl. one of whom reverted to the ranks at his own request for an offence committed during the railway journey.	R
do	20/1/17		Two Lance Corporals were promoted to Corporal.	R

Secret/Confidential

Army Form C. 2118.

Instructions regarding War Diaries and Intelligence
Summaries are contained in F.S. Regs., Part II.
and the Staff Manual respectively. Title pages
will be prepared in manuscript.

WAR DIARY
or
INTELLIGENCE SUMMARY
(Erase heading not required.)

2/1st W.R. FIELD AMBULANCE
ROYAL ARMY MEDICAL CORPS (T.F.)

Place	Date	Hour	Summary of Events and Information	Remarks and references to Appendices
Boffles	20/1/17		1 Private was made Corporal and 6 privates made Lance Corporals (unpaid). Composite section of 3 officers and 66 men were detailed for duty with the 59th Field Ambulance and waited for duty with the ambulance and proceeded to Yiikem le Grand for instructions from the A.D.M.S.	Apt.
do	21/1/17		Preparations made for moving to another area.	Apt.
Map Ref 57D I 10.C.66	22/1/17		Unit less The Composite Section left Boffles at 9-30 A.M. and joined Column of the 183rd Infantry Brigade at Bonnieres. Roads very slippery. Keen frost. Billeting Party of 1 Officer and 20 men proceeded as per instructions. Arrived at Bresle at 4.0 p.m. Encamped under canvas. Arrival reported to Town Major. Have no knowledge of location of Divisional Headquarters. Instructions received (early morning) to proceed to Coignieux	Apt.

Secret Confidential.

Army Form C. 2118.

WAR DIARY
or
INTELLIGENCE SUMMARY.
(Erase heading not required.)

Instructions regarding War Diaries and Intelligence
Summaries are contained in F. S. Regs, Part II.
and the Staff Manual respectively. Title pages
will be prepared in manuscript.

Place	Date	Hour	Summary of Events and Information	Remarks and references to Appendices
Map Ref. 57 D.6.6. I.10.a.	23/2/17		Marching Orders to proceed from Bulot at 10.15 p.m. Orders received to proceed to Bois Labeau. Tedious march. Weather extremely cold. Road surface bad. One shaft of Maltese cart broken owing to horse falling. Load transferred to ambulance wagon. Wagon damaged. cart attached to G.S. wagon. Arrived at Bois Labeau about 5.00 p.m. Took over from 2/M. 56th Fwd Amb. Unable to ascertain location of Divisions Headquarters.	RL
do	24/2/17		Weather extremely cold. Ypt. Bell transferred to No. 3. Canadian Stationary Hospital. 20 cullens suffering from acute nephritis	RL
do	25/2/17		Weather extremely cold. Great difficulty experienced in obtaining fuel.	RL
do	27/2/17		D.D.M.S. 5th Army moved its Camp, and gave verbal instructions for the unit to render medical aid to troops in the vicinity. Detention Hospital of 50 beds for expansion to 100 if necessary. and accommodation	RL
do	29/2/17		Composite Section "A" relieved by Composite Section "B"	RL

Army Form C. 2118.

WAR DIARY
or
INTELLIGENCE SUMMARY.

(Erase heading not required.)

Place	Date	Hour	Summary of Events and Information	Remarks and references to Appendices
Map Ref. 57 D. I.10.C.66.	30/7/17		Instructions received from A.D.M.S. for me to report to 59th Field Ambulance. Capt. Wall left in charge	

S

62nd Division

2/1st W.R. Field Ambulance

140/1994

Feb 1917

COMMITTEE FOR THE
...CAL HISTORY OF THE WAR
Date 4 APR. 1917

WAR DIARY
or
INTELLIGENCE SUMMARY

(Erase heading not required.)

Army Form C. 2118

Vol 2

ORIGINAL

CONFIDENTIAL

WAR DIARY

- OF -

2/1st W.R. FIELD AMBULANCE

FROM 1.2.17 TO 28.2.17

VOL. 2

Army Form C. 2118.

Original

WAR DIARY
or
INTELLIGENCE SUMMARY.
(Erase heading not required.)

Instructions regarding War Diaries and Intelligence Summaries are contained in F.S. Regs., Part II. and the Staff Manual respectively. Title pages will be prepared in manuscript.

Place	Date	Hour	Summary of Events and Information	Remarks and references to Appendices
Bouzaleux	1/9/17		Conditions normal	A
"	2/9/17		Returned from 59th Field Ambulance. Comm.	
"	3/9/17		Composite Section returned from Comm. "C" Section proceeded to Colincamp to took A.D.S. here	A
"	4/9/17		Capt Mackenzie & proceeded to A.D.S. Colincamp and to R.A.P. & Dressing Station in Observation Wood	
"	5/9/17		50 NCO's & men proceeded to Pons for instruction in use of Box Respirator	
"	6/9/17		40 NCO's & men ---- do ---- do ---- do ----	
"	7/9/17		Conditions normal	
"	8/9/17		Four reinforcements arrived	
"	9/9/17		Nothing to report	
"	10/9/17		Two men proceeded to Officers Clearing Hospital Legoncourt to act as Orderlies	

A5834. Wt. W4973/M687. 750,000. 8/16. D. D. & L. Ltd. Forms/C.2118/13.

Army Form C. 2118.

Original

WAR DIARY
or
INTELLIGENCE SUMMARY.
(Erase heading not required.)

Instructions regarding War Diaries and Intelligence Summaries are contained in F. S. Regs., Part II. and the Staff Manual respectively. Title pages will be prepared in manuscript.

2/1 W.R. Fd Ambulance R.A.M.C. (T.F.)

Place	Date	Hour	Summary of Events and Information	Remarks and references to Appendices
Bonleux	11/1/17		One NCO & 2 men M.T. ASC reported for duty.	
"	12/1/17		Conditions normal. Went to ADMS Director. Sent Capt Buckle to ADS really good to relieve Capt Ellison, 1/8 Bn. W. Yorks Regt in orders of ADMS. 1 Officer & 11 other ranks returned from 54th Field Ambulance	
"	13/1/17		One Officer & 18 other ranks proceeded to Berthancourt M.D.S. The Ambulance moved to Berthancourt M.D.S.	
Berthancourt	14/1/17			
"	15/1/17		The Ambulance assisted in work of M.D.S. at Berthancourt prepared to take over.	
"	16/1/17		The Ambulance took over the M.D.S. Berthancourt from the 2/3rd Field Ambulance. 1/Off 56 other ranks proceeded to ADS at Nauby, Maulet & Anchonvillers.	
"	17/1/17		D.D.M.S. visited M.D.S. Berthancourt.	
"	18/1/17		Conditions normal	

Army Form C. 2118.

WAR DIARY
or
INTELLIGENCE SUMMARY.
(Erase heading not required.)

Place	Date	Hour	Summary of Events and Information	Remarks and references to Appendices
Beaucourt	19/1/17		Conditions normal. Visited A.D.M.S. 63rd Division.	
"	20/1/17		Six men returned from the line. Work proceeding satisfactorily.	
"	21/1/17		Visited 71.7 Bde. (Major 57 D.) V Corps M.D.S. to arrange for ambulances to move there.	
Mailly-Maillet	22/1/17		Ambulance moved to Mailly-Maillet, leaving a holding party of 3 officers & 30 other ranks to hand over to incoming Ambulance.	
"	23/1/17		Holding party joined Unit at Mailly-Maillet, having handed over M.D.S. at Beaucourt.	
"	24/1/17		Conditions normal. Men at Auchonvillers relieved & Ambulance detachment established an A.D.S. at Y Ravine	
"	25/1/17		Conditions normal.	
"	26/1/17		D.D.M.S. visited Dressing Station at Mailly-Maillet.	
"	27/1/17		Visited the Advanced Dressing Station, Collecting and Relay Posts.	
"	28/1/17		Conditions normal.	

Mar 1917

S

62nd Div.

140/2042

2/1st W.R. Field Ambulance

COMMITTEE FOR THE
MEDICAL HISTORY OF THE WAR
Date 11 MAY 1917

Army Form C. 2118.

WAR DIARY
or
INTELLIGENCE SUMMARY.

(Erase heading not required.)

—Confidential—

WAR DIARY

of

2/1st West Riding Field Ambulance

From 1st March/17 To 31st March/17.

(Volume III).

Original

Army Form C. 2118.

WAR DIARY
or
INTELLIGENCE SUMMARY.
(Erase heading not required.)

Instructions regarding War Diaries and Intelligence Summaries are contained in F. S. Regs., Part II. and the Staff Manual respectively. Title pages will be prepared in manuscript.

Place	Date	Hour	Summary of Events and Information	Remarks and references to Appendices
Mailly-Mallet.	1.3.17	–	Condition normal. One Officer & detachment established MDS at Q18C2.	A.L.
Q18C21.	2.3.17	–	One Officer & further detachment of the Unit proceeded to MDS. at Q.18.C.2.1. Map 57 D	A.L.
"	3.3.17		Headquarters of Unit transferred. Visited A.D.S. at Luciude Corner & the Culvert	A.L.
"	4.3.17		Visited A.D.M.S. Several Shells were dropped in the vicinity of the M.D.S. about 11.45 a.m.	A.L.
"	5.3.17		Wounded evacuated to CCS by train. More shells were dropped near the MDS at 6.0am and during the night. All work proceeding satisfactorily. The DDMS visited the MDS.	A.L.
"	6.3.17		Germans again shelled this vicinity. The following letter was received from O/C A.D.S. Auchonvillers :– "To O/C 1/1 W.R Field Ambce. Hoy to bring before your notice the conduct of L/Corpl. Hirst who was with me at Auchonvillers. Under heavy shell fire he went out to attend to wounded men at the risk of his own life & did good work afterwards	A.L.

WAR DIARY or INTELLIGENCE SUMMARY

Place	Date	Hour	Summary of Events and Information	Remarks and references to Appendices
Q.(C.)I.	6/3/17		Continued:- in dressing room. He has been extremely useful and his conduct has been excellent. Signed :- R.R.Lloyd Capt. RAMC(T) O/C. 6/R.F. Aube".	
"	7/3/17		Conditions normal. Visited the ADS at Suicide Corner & Kelaven Street. Shells were again dropped in the near vicinity of the M.D.S. & A.D.S.	AL AL
"	8/3/17		Visited the ADS at Suicide Corner. Conditions normal.	AL
"	9/3/17		Conditions normal.	AL
"	10/3/17		Visited the ADS's. Conditions normal. Arrangements being made for evacuation of wounded to CCS by rail.	AL
"	11/3/17		Visited the A.D.S. Regimental Aid Posts & Relay Posts.	AL
"	12/3/17		Conditions normal. Wounded were sent to CCS by train.	AL

Army Form C. 2118.

WAR DIARY
or
INTELLIGENCE SUMMARY.
(Erase heading not required.)

Instructions regarding War Diaries and Intelligence Summaries are contained in F. S. Regs., Part II. and the Staff Manual respectively. Title pages will be prepared in manuscript.

Place	Date	Hour	Summary of Events and Information	Remarks and references to Appendices
Q.18.C.21.	13/3/17		Conditions normal	A1.
"	14/3/17		D.D.M.S. visited the Camp and inspected it, also A.D.S.	A1.
"	15/3/17		Visited A.D.M.S. 62nd Division	
"	16/3/17		Two bearer Sub-divisions arrived. One sent forward to A.D.S, the Second being retained at M.D.S. for emergencies	A1.
"	17/3/17		Conditions normal	A2.
"	18/3/17		A.D.M.S. visited the M.D.S, A.D.S, Relay Posts etc.	A2.
"	19/3/17		Conditions normal	A2.
"	20/3/17		Visited the A.D.M.S. 62nd Division	A2.

Army Form C. 2118.

WAR DIARY
or
INTELLIGENCE SUMMARY.
(Erase heading not required.)

Instructions regarding War Diaries and Intelligence Summaries are contained in F. S. Regs., Part II. and the Staff Manual respectively. Title pages will be prepared in manuscript.

Place	Date	Hour	Summary of Events and Information	Remarks and references to Appendices
Q18C21	21/3/17		Visited the ADSs, Relay Posts etc.	A
"	22/3/17		ADS established at G2D28 which I inspected	A
"	23/3/17		Conditions normal	A
"	24/3/17		Visited ADSs 62nd Division. Conditions normal	A
"	25/3/17		Inspected all ADSs, Relay Posts	A
"	26/3/17		Conditions normal. Visited ADSs.	A
"	27/3/17		Arrangements made to recall all attached personnel.	A
"	28/3/17		Conditions normal. DDMS visited the ADSs	A

WAR DIARY
or
INTELLIGENCE SUMMARY.

(Erase heading not required.)

Army Form C. 2118.

Place	Date	Hour	Summary of Events and Information	Remarks and references to Appendices
Q18C.2.1	24/3/17		Conditions normal. Invited A.D.M.S. 62nd Division	A1
"	26/3/17		Invited all A.D.S.; Relay posts etc.	A1
"	31/3/17		Conditions normal.	A1

Walter Lister
LIEUT COL. R.A.M.C. (T)
2/1st W.R. FIELD AMBULANCE
ROYAL ARMY MEDICAL CORPS (T.F.)

Army Form C. 2118.

WAR DIARY
or
INTELLIGENCE SUMMARY.

(Erase heading not required.)

Instructions regarding War Diaries and Intelligence Summaries are contained in F. S. Regs., Part II. and the Staff Manual respectively. Title pages will be prepared in manuscript.

Place	Date	Hour	Summary of Events and Information	Remarks and references to Appendices

"Abdomen"

S—

Gunshot

21st West Riding F.A.

140/086

COMMITTEE FOR THE
MEDICAL HISTORY OF THE WAR
Date -6 JUN.1917

"ORIGINAL"

Army Form C. 2118.

WAR DIARY
or
INTELLIGENCE SUMMARY.
(Erase heading not required.)

Instructions regarding War Diaries and Intelligence Summaries are contained in F. S. Regs., Part II. and the Staff Manual respectively. Title pages will be prepared in manuscript.

Place	Date	Hour	Summary of Events and Information	Remarks and references to Appendices

Vol 4

Confidential.

WAR DIARY

of

2/1st W.R. FIELD AMBULANCE
ROYAL ARMY MEDICAL CORPS (T.F.)

From 1st April 1917 To 30th April 1917.

Volume IV.

ORIGINAL

WAR DIARY or INTELLIGENCE SUMMARY.

Army Form C. 2118.

(Erase heading not required.)

Instructions regarding War Diaries and Intelligence Summaries are contained in F.S. Regs., Part II. and the Staff Manual respectively. Title pages will be prepared in manuscript.

Place	Date	Hour	Summary of Events and Information	Remarks and references to Appendices
Q18 C2.1	1/4/17		Orders received to take over from 9/o. L.S.R. Field Ambce at Lancashire Dump. Party despatched for this purpose. Visited the place & made all necessary arrangements for reception of C.P.S within from A.D.S's Relay Posts with the exception of [also personnel & equipment] at G2D. & h Lancashire Dump D.R.S. taken over	R.A.M.C. 3rd rue Dir. Orders N° 9.
Lancashire Dump	2/4/17		Headquarters of Unit moved to Lancashire Dump. A.D.M.S. visited the Dil. Rest Station there. Arrangements completed and all branches of duties working satisfactorily. A.D.M.S. instructed that Capt. Pope be temporarily attached to 9/o. L.S.R Field Ambce.	A.D.M.S. Letter of 2/4/1917
"	3/4/17		Conditions normal. Capt. Whitelaw detailed to act as M.O. I/e 1/4th Batt. W. Yorks Regt. One bearer Sub-division of the Unit ord for duty to 9/o. L.S.R. Ambce – also 1 Ford & 4 Daimler Motor Ambces.	A.D.M.S. wire M/5A A.D.M.S. wire 71/142
"	4/4/17		Instructions received from A.D.M.S. to send a Bed bearer Sub-division & 9/o. L.S.R.7. Ambce at to take a third Sub-division in readiness. This was complied with. Condition normal.	A.D.M.S. wire no. 116/A

WAR DIARY
or
INTELLIGENCE SUMMARY.
(Erase heading not required.)

Army Form C. 2118.

Instructions regarding War Diaries and Intelligence Summaries are contained in F. S. Regs., Part II. and the Staff Manual respectively. Title pages will be prepared in manuscript.

Place	Date	Hour	Summary of Events and Information	Remarks and references to Appendices
Q35.D.28	5/4/17		Conditions normal. Orders received for Capt Robinson to proceed to S/B 48th for temporary duty. Complied with and also sent eight more bearers. Orders received at 10 pm. to send a further Medical Officer to 1/2 Lo.R.M.A. for temporary duty. Capt Pickles instructed to join by 12 noon of 6th inst. Three Mark VI Ambulances, & horses & each also sent to arrive by noon of the 6th inst.	ADMS letter M/2024/1. ADMS wire num 8 of 5/4/1/1
	6/4/17.		Conditions normal. Capt Pickles returned to MDS Q.16.C.V.1. for duty on verbal instructions of ADMS. Instructions received to run Q.18.C.V. as a Car Station Only.	ADMS letter M/057.
	7/4/17.		Conditions normal. Capt Pier Le proceeded to join 1/8 Bar. Works Regt. for duty as RMO vice Capt Wall who has received instructions from Army Land Div. to report to MDS at 1/1 A.b.u.	M/154.
	8/4/17.		Capt Pickles returned to Unit on verbal instructions of CO/ADMS 62nd Division.	
	9/4/17.		Nothing to report.	

WAR DIARY
or
INTELLIGENCE SUMMARY.
(Erase heading not required.)

Army Form C. 2118.

Instructions regarding War Diaries and Intelligence Summaries are contained in F.S. Regs., Part II. and the Staff Manual respectively. Title pages will be prepared in manuscript.

Place	Date	Hour	Summary of Events and Information	Remarks and references to Appendices
Q.35.D.2.8	10/4/17		One Officer and 5 other ranks sent to H/149.L.8.b take over from P.D.T. on instructions from A.D.M.S. 62nd Division	ADMS wire M140
"	11/4/17		One officer with bearer Sub division sent to assist 7/2 W.R. Field Ambce at Bouzellers. One Section of 7/2 Home Counties Field Amb arrived to take over D.R.S. ADMS 58th Divn marked the D.R.S.	ADMS wire M>>>uu
"	12/4/17		Loading equipment. Nothing to report	
"	13/4/17		ADMS 62nd Divmn marked the D.R.S. Ambulance moved to proceed to H/149.6.8 billeting for the night at Miraumont. Instructions to take over from P.D.T. Cancelled. The Ambulance Camped at G.9.B.b.3. near Achiet-le-Grand. Capt Robinson rejoined Unit (Sick) from 7/2 W.R. Field Ambce	ADMS wire J.M. 383
G.9.B.b.3	14/4/17		Capt Mackenzie relieved Capt Robinson at 7/2 W.R. Field Ambce	—do— ADMS wire M14
"	15/4/17		Gas Alert on. The D.M.S. V Corps visited the Camp. ADMS 62nd Division visited the Camp.	
"	16/4/17		Gas Alert off. ADMS 62nd Division visited the Camp	

Army Form C. 2118.

WAR DIARY
or
INTELLIGENCE SUMMARY.
(Erase heading not required.)

Instructions regarding War Diaries and Intelligence Summaries are contained in F. S. Regs., Part II. and the Staff Manual respectively. Title pages will be prepared in manuscript.

Place	Date	Hour	Summary of Events and Information	Remarks and references to Appendices
G9.B.b.3	18/4/17		Nothing to report.	
-"-	19/4/17		ADMS visited the Camp.	
-"-	20/4/17		ADMS visited the Camp. I visited ADMS and agreed upon site for Ambulance Hospital	
-"-	21/4/17		Conference at ADMS office 10-30am. sent a N.C.O. to told ground for new Camp	
-"-	22/4/17		ADMS 62nd Division visited the Camp. Sent a party to new camp to clean ground.	
-"-	23/4/17		Nothing to report. Visited ADMS 62nd Division.	
-"-	24/4/17		Advance party proceeded to new Camp. Motor lorry transported several loads.	
H.Dg7	25/4/17		The Ambulance moved today to new camp at Map 57c Gordon 2. H1d9.7	

T2134. Wt. W708—776. 500000. 4/15. Sir J. C. & S.

Army Form C. 2118.

WAR DIARY
or
INTELLIGENCE SUMMARY.
(Erase heading not required.)

Place	Date	Hour	Summary of Events and Information	Remarks and references to Appendices
H.I.D.9	26/4/17		New Camp Planned. Nothing to report. ADMS 62nd Division visited the Camp. Lieut Bannock reported for duty.	ADMS letter 2692/1.
"	27/4/17		D.D.M.S. V Corps visited and inspected the Camp. Capt. Robinson returned to duty.	
"	28/4/17		Joined the ADMS, 62nd Division.	
"	29/4/17		Nothing to report. Capt Locklin returned to duty; L/Cpl Boburn Hunt awarded the Military Medal.	Corps MM No 316 & 3785 28/4/17
"	30/4/17		Joined ADMS, 62nd Division	

May 1917

62nd Div
14/2/16/

2/1st West Riding F.A.

COMMITTEE FOR THE
MEDICAL HISTORY OF THE WAR
Date 10 JUL. 1917

Army Form C. 2118.

WAR DIARY
or
INTELLIGENCE SUMMARY.

Vol 5

ORIGINAL.

Confidential

WAR DIARY
— of —
2/1st West Riding F. Amb^ce
From May 1st 1917 To May 31st 1917.
Volume 5.

Army Form C. 2118.

WAR DIARY
or
INTELLIGENCE SUMMARY.
(Erase heading not required.)

Instructions regarding War Diaries and Intelligence Summaries are contained in F.S. Regs., Part II. and the Staff Manual respectively. Title pages will be prepared in manuscript.

Place	Date	Hour	Summary of Events and Information	Remarks and references to Appendices
H.I.D.97	1/5/17		Invited A.D.M.S. 62nd Division.	
"	2/5/17		Orders received to hold one Beaver Sub. division at Cocey 8/2nd LSR. 4. Aubee and to accommodate one Beaver Sub-division 53 5/3rd LSR.7. Aubee as reinforcement to 1/2 LSR7. Aubee.	ADMS Leper No.79/11/5 2/5/17
"	3/5/17	6.15 am	Beaver Sub. division of the Unit proceeded to Turlingo duty 2oth to LSR7. Aubee and Beaver Sub. division of 1/2 LSR7 Aubee followed at 11.15 am. Orders received from ADMS. 62nd Div to have a third that Beaver Sub-division in readiness.	ADMS Leper dated 3/5/17
"	4/5/17		ADMS. 62nd Division visited the Camp	
"	5/5/17		Notification received that 1235 Pte 4/1 Pratt & 10612 Pte ? Fowler killed in action. Koden.	
"	6/5/17		No.999 Pte Sadler killed today, 1864 Pte Tosbey & 251 Pte Lees wounded.	
"	7/5/17		All personnel attached to 1/2 and 1/3 LSR7. Aubee returned to unit today.	No 2968 ADMS letter

T.J.184. Wt. W708-776. 500000. 4/15. Sir J. C. & S.

Army Form C. 2118.

WAR DIARY
or
INTELLIGENCE SUMMARY.
(Erase heading not required.)

Instructions regarding War Diaries and Intelligence Summaries are contained in F.S. Regs., Part II. and the Staff Manual respectively. Title pages will be prepared in manuscript.

Place	Date	Hour	Summary of Events and Information	Remarks and references to Appendices
H.Dq.7	8/5/17		A.D.M.S. 62nd Division visited the Camp.	
-"-	9/5/17		Capt. Mackenzie Robinson returned to Unit from 23rd C.C.S.	
-"-	10/5/17		Capt. Brown proceeded relieve Capt. A.J. Wells 7/5. K.O.Y.L.I., who joined the Unit temporarily.	Casualties M.D.7/19.5.17
-"-	11/5/17		A.D.M.S. visited the Camp	
-"-	12/5/17		62nd Div. Medical Arrangements Nos 1. & V Corps Medical Arrangements No 24 instructing this Unit to take over Field Ambulance Site at Courcelles.	
-"-	13/5/17		Arrangement made with O.C. 2/2nd Field Amb. to move at 10.0 a.m. on the 14th inst.	
Courcelles	14/5/17		Move completed by 10.0 a.m Ambulance Established at Courcelles.	
-"-	15/5/17		Capt. Pope returned to the Unit from Mo Stay. Capt. Mackenzie reported to M.D.S. Monchy for duty as instructed in	

Army Form C. 2118.

WAR DIARY
or
INTELLIGENCE SUMMARY.
(Erase heading not required.)

Instructions regarding War Diaries and Intelligence Summaries are contained in F. S. Regs., Part II. and the Staff Manual respectively. Title pages will be prepared in manuscript.

Place	Date	Hour	Summary of Events and Information	Remarks and references to Appendices
Courcelles	15/5/17		RAMC 62nd Divn Order No 72.	
"	16/5/17		Sergt Knagg of this Unit recommended for good work by Capt J Bateton. Motor Bath Works Regt. Letter received from O.C. 2nd LSR & Ambce expressing his appreciation of the work done by the personnel of this ambulance attached to the 2nd LSR & Ambce.	Cons Letter
"	17/5/17		A.D.M.S. 62nd Division visited the Camp. Instructions received to hold 2 brass sub-divisions two officers or orderly to LSR & Ambce	7h 335 of 15 Cons Letter 7h 335 of 17/5
"	18/5/17		Divisional sick admitted to this hospital.	
"	19/5/17		2nd re-inforcements arrived this day.	
"	20/5/17		Conference of Medical Officers at Office of A.D.M.S. 62nd Divn which I attended. D.D.M.S. V Corps visited the Camp & Hospital	
"	21/5/17		A.D.M.S. 62nd Division visited the Camp & Hospital.	

Army Form C. 2118.

WAR DIARY
or
INTELLIGENCE SUMMARY.
(Erase heading not required.)

Instructions regarding War Diaries and Intelligence Summaries are contained in F. S. Regs., Part II. and the Staff Manual respectively. Title pages will be prepared in manuscript.

Place	Date	Hour	Summary of Events and Information	Remarks and references to Appendices
Courcelles	22/3/17		DDMS V Corps visited the Camp. Hospital extended	
-	23/3/17		Asst Office Audit of accounts for period Oct/14 to Dec/16 received. I mailed ADMS 62nd Division	
-	24/3/17		One NCO & 12 men proceeded to MDS. More today. ADMS 62nd Division visited the Camp.	Instructions re ADMS 62nd Div.
-	25/3/17		DDMS V Corps visited the Camp. Enemy Aeroplane over the Camp 11.05pm. Several bombs dropped in the district. Nothing to report.	
-	26/3/17			
-	27/3/17		ADMS inspected the Camp and Hospital. Evacuation arrangements No 13 & V Corps Medical arrangements received instructing the time to take over from the 2nd Field Amber, Achiet-le-Grand on to below the Boyh line. Sergt H Knapp awarded Military Medal	DRO No 5594 26/3/1917
-	28/3/17		Inspected the Site of the 22nd Field Amber rearranged on this Unit to exchange sites with them at 10am 30/3/17	

WAR DIARY
or
INTELLIGENCE SUMMARY.
(Erase heading not required.)

Army Form C. 2118.

Place	Date	Hour	Summary of Events and Information	Remarks and references to Appendices
Corcelles	28/3/17	Contd	Regulated that personnel attached to Field Ambulance of the 58th Division be returned. Gave Div. Medical arrangements No 74 received instructing the Unit to take Sick of 185th & 186th Infantry Brigades when moves have been completed.	
–	29/3/17		Letter received from OC 2/2nd A.C. Field Amb. reporting on Capt Mackenzie's excellent services during the period he was attached to them.	
G9.A.10.8	30/3/17		The Unit moved to new Site at Echelet-le-Grand and opened Hospital for Sick. Letter received from ADMS 59th Division expressing his appreciation of work performed by all ranks of the Unit during the time they were at the M.D.S. Mory. ADC attached returned to Unit today.	
–	31/3/17		Hospital in efficient working order. 185th & 186th Infantry Brigade Sick Collected by Ambulance Cars. ADMS 62nd Division visited the Camp.	

Noel Lister
LIEUT-COL., R.A.M.C.
2/1st W.R. FIELD AMBULANCE
ROYAL ARMY MEDICAL CORPS (T.F.)

COMMITTEE FOR THE
MEDICAL HISTORY OF THE WAR

Date - 7 AUG. 1917

Army Form C. 2118.

WAR DIARY
or
INTELLIGENCE SUMMARY.
(Erase heading not required.)

ORIGINAL

— Confidential —

— WAR DIARY —

of

2/1st West Riding Field Ambulance

From 1st June To June 30th
1917

Vol: 6

Army Form C. 2118.

WAR DIARY
or
INTELLIGENCE SUMMARY.
(Erase heading not required.)

Instructions regarding War Diaries and Intelligence Summaries are contained in F. S. Regs., Part II. and the Staff Manual respectively. Title pages will be prepared in manuscript.

Place	Date	Hour	Summary of Events and Information	Remarks and references to Appendices
Map 57c. Gq.b.2.7.	1-6-17		Invited the ADMS 62nd Division.	
"	2-6-17		Attended Conference at office of ADMS 62nd Division	
"	3-6-17		DDMS V Corps visited the Hospital and Camp. ADMS 62nd Division also visited the Camp	
"	4-6-17		Nothing to report	
"	5-6-17		Nothing to report	
"	6-6-17		Attended Conference of M.O. at the office of the ADMS 62nd Division. Capt. C.P. Snow RAMC(T) joined 2/1st West Riding Regt to act as Reg'l M.O. during absence on leave of Capt. Havelock RAMC(T)	ADMS letter No M/3991 dated 5/6/17
"	7-6-17		Invited the ADMS 62nd Division.	
"	8-6-17		ADMS 62nd Division inspected the Ambulance (including A.S.C. attached) & expressed his approval. Capt. R.A. MacKenzie proceeded to DDMS V Corps Hd. qrs. in temporary ADMS to L Corps Army Troops	ADMS letter No M/4011 dated 8/6/17

Army Form C. 2118.

WAR DIARY
or
INTELLIGENCE SUMMARY.
(Erase heading not required.)

Instructions regarding War Diaries and Intelligence Summaries are contained in F. S. Regs., Part II. and the Staff Manual respectively. Title pages will be prepared in manuscript.

Place	Date	Hour	Summary of Events and Information	Remarks and references to Appendices
Maps 57C G.B.7.	9/6/17		ADMS 62nd Division invited the Camp. Capt Brooks RAMC(T) relieved Capt Cobron an temporary MO to 2/6 W.Riding Regt. Capt Brown returned to Units sick	ADMS letter My 9022 d. 2/5/17
-"-	10/6/17		ADMS, V Corps invited the Camp	
-"-	11/6/17		Invited ADMS 62nd Division	
-"-	12/6/17		Nothing to report	
-"-	13/6/17		Nothing to report	
-"-	14/6/17		Medical Board on P.B. men	
-"-	15/6/17		Capt. Brown. RAMC(T) proceeded Onvieux to sit on Medical Board on P.B. men. ADMS invited the Camp. GOC Division and staff inspected the Transport, Camp, Hospital of this Unit. Expressed his complete satisfaction and approval	
-"-	16/6/17		Invited ADMS. 62nd Division	

Soralee ADMS 62nd Division

WAR DIARY
or
INTELLIGENCE SUMMARY

Army Form C. 2118.

(Erase heading not required.)

Instructions regarding War Diaries and Intelligence Summaries are contained in F.S. Regs., Part II. and the Staff Manual respectively. Title pages will be prepared in manuscript.

Place	Date	Hour	Summary of Events and Information	Remarks and references to Appendices
Map 57c G.9.B.27.	17/6/17	18h/17	Visited A.D.M.S. 62nd Divn. Attended Court of enquiry at 43rd Casy Clg.	
"		18h/17	Nothing to report. A.D.M.S. 62nd Division visited the Camp.	
"	19/6/17		Capt. E.S. Brown, R.A.M.C.(T) joined 2/5 B. West Riding Regt. to act as temporary Regt. M.O. during absence on leave of Capt. W. Robertson R.A.M.C.(T) D.M.S. Third Army, D.D.M.S. V Corps, A.D.M.S. 62nd Division inspected the Hospital and Camp. The D.M.S. Third Army expressed his satisfaction and stated that he was much pleased with the arrangements of the Hospital and Camp in General.	A.D.M.S. letter 19/4/17 dated 9/6/17.
"	20/6/17		Nothing to report.	
"	21/6/17		Lieut. S.O. Pruitt, U.S.M.C. posted to this Unit for duty.	A.D.M.S. 09/360 22.6.17.
"	22/6/17		I visited A.D.M.S. 62nd Divn. Capt. Blackburn, Lieut. McD. Lawson & myself visited 61st Field Amb. at H.B.4y5 One NCO & eight men proceeded to A.D.S. Truth Ret. C.29.a.5.0. to improve rds. Capt. J.R. Blackburn & Capt. J.H.D. Gartside visited A.D.S. Truth Rt. C.29.a.5.0.	Medical Arrangements No. 12
"	23/6/17		Capt. J.H. Blackburn, Capt. H.D. Ryselas, 2 NCOs & 38 men proceeded to the A.D.S. Met. Ref. C.29.a.5.0. ample rds review to relieving garrison of R.A.Ps. Map References: C.23.d.6.9., C.24.d.8.5. C.30.a.8.5. A.D.S. Truth Rt. C.29.a.5.0. & Loading Point C.26.d. Central.	
"	24/6/17		A.D.M.S. 62nd Divn. visited the Camp. Party of 10 men returned from Rest Camp at St. Vaabry Sur Somme. Party of 4 men proceeded to Rest Camp at St. Vaabry Sur Somme.	A.D.M.S. 09/425 dated 6.17

Army Form C. 2118.

WAR DIARY
or
INTELLIGENCE SUMMARY.
(Erase heading not required.)

Instructions regarding War Diaries and Intelligence Summaries are contained in F. S. Regs., Part II. and the Staff Manual respectively. Title pages will be prepared in manuscript.

Place	Date	Hour	Summary of Events and Information	Remarks and references to Appendices
G.9.A.2.Y.	25/6/17		1 N.C.O. & 5 men proceeded to M.D.S. Mass Rgt. H.16.d.Y.5. to take over from 6/0t Field Amb. 20th Division. Ford Car returned 6/0t Field Amb. (Col. Honey) reported to take over M.D.S. at C.26.d central. 1 Officer & party from 6/0t Field Amb. (Col. Honey) reported to take over M.D.S. at G.9.0.7. Capt. 26 Lt. Robinson returned from leave.	H V. Corps Memo No. 3 appx x
H.16.d.Y.5.	26/6/17		Remainder of the Unit proceeded to Rennes at 10 a.m. to H.16.d.Y.5. Leave 3 N.C.O. & 2 Men reserved at G.9.2.4. as Rear Party. Carrying ground to huts very bad. Cook-house roof of the road. Relief completed with exception of holding Party at G.9.2.2.Y. Capt. J.A. Mackenzie appointed Military Comm. A.D.M.S. 20th Division worked Camp.	H DRa 6/8 25/6/14 H H
"	27/6/17		A.D.M.S. 20th Division visited Camp. A.D.M.S. 62nd Division visited Camp.	H
"	28/6/17		First half relief carried out. (22 men)	H
"	29/6/17		Men relieved reported at M.D.S. H.16.d.Y.5. A.D.M.S. 62nd Division worked Camp. (2 men)	H
"	30/6/17		Water Cart returned from 23rd Field Amb. (V. Corps Reg. Para)	H

Walter Lake
LIEUT-COL. R.A.M.O.
2/1st W.R. FIELD AMBULANCE
ROYAL ARMY MEDICAL CORPS (T.)

2/1st West Riding F.A.

COMMITTEE FOR THE
MEDICAL HISTORY OF THE WAR
Date 10 SEP. 1917

ORIGINAL.

WAR DIARY
or
INTELLIGENCE SUMMARY.

Army Form C. 2118.

Vol 7

Confidential

WAR DIARY

of

Lieut. Colonel WALTER LISTER,
R.A.M.C.(T)

Commdg. 2/1st West Riding Field Ambce.

for the month of JULY 1917

Army Form C. 2118.

WAR DIARY
or
INTELLIGENCE SUMMARY.
(Erase heading not required.)

Instructions regarding War Diaries and Intelligence Summaries are contained in F. S. Regs., Part II. and the Staff Manual respectively. Title pages will be prepared in manuscript.

Place	Date	Hour	Summary of Events and Information	Remarks and references to Appendices
M.D.S. H.I.S.D.A.S.	1/4/17		Nothing to report.	
"	2/4/17		D.D.M.S. V Corps visited the Camp.	
"	3/4/17		A.D.M.S. 62nd Division visited the Camp. Five cars from the 36th M.A.C. attached to this Unit.	
"	4/4/17		I attended a Conference at the A.D.M.S.'s Office.	
"			Five cars (36th M.A.C.) transferred to the 2/3rd West Riding Field Ambulance in accordance with instructions from the A.D.M.S. 62nd Division.	
"	5/4/17		I interviewed O.C. 62nd Divisional Train A.S.C. in reference to Officers. Sent Lt. Col. C Whonnes, A.D.M.S. 62nd Division marked the Camp.	
"	6/4/17		I marked A.D.S. Trap Ry. C.27.a.5.0. Capt. C.S. Brown R.A.M.C (T) Rejoined the Unit after being duty as Adjutant to the O.C. of the 2/5th West Riding Regt. A.D.V.S. inspected horses and mules. Capt. H.B. Pope R.P.M.C.T. found myself harassed A.S.C Officer as to them failure of being transferred out the infantry.	

A834 Wt. W4973 M687 750,000 8/16 D. D. & L. Ltd. Forms/C.2118/13.

Army Form C. 2118.

WAR DIARY
or
INTELLIGENCE SUMMARY.
(Erase heading not required.)

Place	Date	Hour	Summary of Events and Information	Remarks and references to Appendices
Staff S/C H.16.d.7.5.	1/4/17		One Yest. Col. Division (concluding a Medical Officer i.e Lieut. S.O. PRUITT. U.S.M.C.) proceeded to No. 45 C.C.S. for temporary duty in respect of similar personnel of the 56th Division. Capt. L.A. MacKenzie proceeded to the 161 Reserve Park for temporary duty as Medical Officer to that Unit.	A.D.M.S. 8 R.M.S. 2/9/17 G2 A.D.M.S. 14/9/17 92 2/7/17
"	2/4/17		Two men returned from the Rest Camp, St. VALERY-SUR-SOMME.	G2
"	3/4/17		Lieut. W.E. LARSON and myself visited the D.D.S. Maj. Gen. C. 29 a.50.	G2
"	4/4/17		Nothing to report.	G2
"	5/4/17		Lieut. Col. C.W. EAMES a/A.D.M.S. 62nd Div. invited to Camp.	G2
"	6/4/17		Nothing to report.	G2

WAR DIARY
INTELLIGENCE SUMMARY
(Erase heading not required.)

Army Form C. 2118.

Instructions regarding War Diaries and Intelligence Summaries are contained in F. S. Regs., Part II. and the Staff Manual respectively. Title pages will be prepared in manuscript.

Place	Date	Hour	Summary of Events and Information	Remarks and references to Appendices
Araf. s/fc A.16.d.7.5.	13/7/17		Nothing to report.	
"	14/7/17		Five reinforcements joined the Unit. Capt. C. B. Rose and party proceeded for duty up the Line in relief of Capt. G. W. B. Holtman and party. Capt. L. A. Mackenzie rejoined the Unit after doing duty as Medical Officer with the 46th Reserve Park.	A.D.M.S. 2/0000 23/7/17
"	15/7/17		Capt. J. H. Blackburn and party returned to the M.D.S. Mons Rd. A.15.d.7.5. after doing duty up the Lines. Lieut. Col. Eaves C.M.G. D.D.M.S. 62nd Div. visited the Camp.	
"	16/7/17		Lay men proceeded early morning to report to M.O.'s i/c Duke of Wellington's Regt. Various C.R.E. &Y. for temporary duty.	
"	17/7/17		A.D.M.S. 62nd Division inspected the Camp.	A.D.M.S. 2/0000 23/7/17

WAR DIARY or INTELLIGENCE SUMMARY.

Army Form C. 2118.

(Erase heading not required.)

Place	Date	Hour	Summary of Events and Information	Remarks and references to Appendices
Amp S/C H.16.d.7.5.	18/7/17		A.O.C. 62nd Division visited the Camp and inspected the telephones. A.D.M.S. 62nd Division visited the Camp.	
"	19/7/17		A.D.M.S. 62nd Div. and myself proceeded to the A.D.S. Trey Pet C.29.a.5.0.	
"	20/7/17		D.D.M.S. VI Corps visited the Camp, also A.D.M.S. 62nd Div.	
"	21/7/17		1 N.C.O. and 19 Other ranks detailed for temporary procedure only morning. Capt. B.W. Robinson proceeded for temporary duty on Medical Officer to 2/7th Bn. West York Regt. in relief of Capt. V. Whitelaw. Capt. C.S. Brown proceeded to the A.D.S. Trey Pet C.29.a.5.0. Capt. H.G. Pickles	22/7/17 20/7/17
	22/7/17		Capt. H.G. Pickles returned to the M.D.S. from Pet H.16.a.7.5. after being duty at the A.D.S. Trey Pet C.29.a.5.0.	
	23/7/17		Capt. H.G. Pickles and one N.C.O. reported at the Divisional Gas School, Favreuil, to attend a course assembling at 4 p.m.	

WAR DIARY
INTELLIGENCE SUMMARY

Army Form C. 2118.

Place	Date	Hour	Summary of Events and Information	Remarks and references to Appendices
M.a.b. 54 C. H.16.d.y.5.	24/9/17		Nothing to report	
"	25/9/17		A.D.M.S. 62nd Div. visited the Camp. Lieut. Col. Davidson (including Lieut. P.O. PRUITT. U.S.M.C.) reported to Unit at H.16.d.y.5. after going through No.45 C.C.S.	
"	26/9/17		Nothing to report	
"	27/9/17		A.D.M.S. VI Corps visited the Camp and inspected the establishment with camp. O.D.M.S. visited the Camp. 1 N.C.O and 12 men proceeded for duty with the line in relief. Capt. 86.9 Bickler and one N.C.O. regraded their unit after attending a course at the Divisional Gas School, FAREUIL.	
"	28/9/17		1 N.C.O and 12 men returned to the M.D.S. Gard. Ref. H.16.d.y.5 after going through the line.	
"	29/9/17		Capt. Mackenzie and one S/Sgt proceeded unemployed now in the VI Corps Change Corp and. that Pte/6vc B.20.C.2.Y. Lieut. S.O. PRUITT. U.S.M.C. proceeded to DUNKERQUE on duty.	

WAR DIARY
INTELLIGENCE SUMMARY

Army Form C. 2118.

Place	Date	Hour	Summary of Events and Information	Remarks and references to Appendices
Mob S.C. H.Q. 4 F.A.	2/9/17		Capt L.A. Mackenzie, 1 N.C.O. and 1 man proceeded to the Divisional Horse Standing Ground in order to arrived in two convoys on July 3/9/17. Lieut. Col. Foss A.D.V.S. and the A.D.M.S. 62nd Div. visited the Camp on July Lieutenant Evans D.A.L. Gallane, C.B., D.S.O. Commanding VI Corps visited the Horse lines of this Unit, and expressed his satisfaction with the condition of animals.	
"	3/9/17		A.D.M.S. 62nd Division visited the Camp. Cpl. J.E. Fitch A.S.C. attached, proceeded to FORGES LES EAUX to attend Veterinary Course.	

Rachulale
LIEUT-COOL, R.A.M.C. (T)
2/1st V.R. FIELD AMBULANCE
ROYAL ARMY MEDICAL CORPS (T.F.)

140/2264

2/1 F. West Riding F.A.

COMMITTEE FOR THE
MEDICAL HISTORY OF THE WAR
Date -1 OCT.1917

WAR DIARY or INTELLIGENCE SUMMARY.

Army Form C. 2118.

Vol 8

ORIGINAL

— Confidential —

— WAR DIARY —
— of —
2/1st W.R. Field Ambulance —

— Period 1st to 31st Aug./17.

Volume VIII

Army Form C. 2118.

WAR DIARY
or
INTELLIGENCE SUMMARY.
(Erase heading not required.)

Instructions regarding War Diaries and Intelligence Summaries are contained in F.S. Regs., Part II. and the Staff Manual respectively. Title pages will be prepared in manuscript.

Place	Date	Hour	Summary of Events and Information	Remarks and references to Appendices
Infield H16 D 7.5. Map 57c.	1917 Aug 1		Nothing to report.	
"	- 2		Capt Mackenzie. R.A.M.C.(T) + one N.C.O. + one man returned from Div. Gas School, Taneuil.	
"	- 3		Capt. Pope reported to Headquarters Unit. A.D.M.S. visited the Camp. Capt Pickles. R.A.M.C.(T) proceeded for temporary duty with 319th Bde. R.F.A.	A.D.M.S. M/5331 of 31/7/1916
"	- 4		Capt. Robinson. R.A.M.C.(T) rejoined Unit after temporary duty with 2/7th Battn. W. Yorks Regt. A.D.M.S. visited the Camp.	
"	- 5		Medical Board held on personnel of VI Corps Salvage Co. - President Lieut.- Col. Lister - Member Capt. Mackenzie. One N.C.O. & 5 men proceeded to Summer Rest Camp, St. Valery	
"	- 6		A.D.M.S. visited the Camp. Staff- Capt Lloyd visited the Camp.	6 radion R.A.M.C. order No. 16.
"	- 7		Capt. Pope Franty proceeded to A.D.S	

WAR DIARY or INTELLIGENCE SUMMARY

Army Form C. 2118.

(Erase heading not required.)

Place	Date 1917	Hour	Summary of Events and Information	Remarks and references to Appendices
Map 57C. H1b. D.7.s	Aug 8		Capt. Brown R.A.M.C.(T) and party returned from A.D.S. to M.D.S. after being relieved by 8th Field Ambulance. Brig-Genl. De Falbe visited the Camp.	6 mo Diar RAMC Order No.16.
"	- 9		D.D.M.S, VI Corps visited the Camp accompanied by A.D.M.S.	
"	- 10		Capt. Mackenzie. R.A.M.C.(T) attended meeting at No. 3. C.C.S on "Study of Shell Shock"	A.D.M.S. M5393 of 3/8/17
"	- 11		Capt. C.S. Brown R.A.M.C.(T) proceeded to 2/5th Batt. Works Regt. for Temporary duty. One N.C.O. & 19 men detailed for haymaking. returned to Unit.	A.D.M.S. M5533 of 9/8/17
"	- 12		A.D.M.S. visited the Camp	
"	- 13		D.M.S. IIIrd Army inspected the Camp. Remarked "very good Shows & very creditable". A.D.M.S visited the Camp.	
"	- 14		A.D.M.S lectured the M.O's on "Surgical Shock".	
"	- 15		Nothing to report.	
"	- 16		Capt. Pickles. R.A.M.C.(T) returned to Unit from 313th Bde R.F.A.	

WAR DIARY
or
INTELLIGENCE SUMMARY.
(Erase heading not required.)

Army Form C. 2118.

Instructions regarding War Diaries and Intelligence Summaries are contained in F. S. Regs, Part II. and the Staff Manual respectively. Title pages will be prepared in manuscript.

Place	Date	Hour	Summary of Events and Information	Remarks and references to Appendices
57.C. H16D7.S.	1917 Aug 17		A.D.M.S. visited the Camp.	
"	-18		VI Corps Horse Show. This Unit obtained the following:- 3rd Prize for Motor Ambce Turnout. Highly Commended for Horse Ambce Turnout.	
"	-19		D.A.D.M.S. and myself visited the forward area and A.D.S. etc. N.C.O & party proceeded to Rest Camp, St Valery-sur-Somme. A.D.M.S. inspected Horses. One N.C.O & party returned from St Valery Rest Camp.	
"	-20		Capt. Mackenzie reported to A.D.M.S. for instruction. Two men reported to Field Ambulance of 42nd Division to act as holding party.	
"	-21		Nothing to report.	
"	-22		Nothing to report.	
"	-23		Capt. Mackenzie proceeded to Dans. Haze. A.D.M.S. visited the Camp.	

WAR DIARY
or
INTELLIGENCE SUMMARY.

(Erase heading not required.)

Army Form C. 2118.

Place	Date 1917	Hour	Summary of Events and Information	Remarks and references to Appendices
57C. H1b.D.7.S.	Aug 24		A.D.M.S. visited the Camp. Capt Pope returned from A.D.S. prior to proceeding on leave.	
"	-25		A.D.M.S. & Capt. Pope examined water supply in the forward area. Medical Board held on personnel of No 2 P.B. Labour Coy.	
"	-26		Capt Pickles R.A.M.C (T) proceeded to 2/6th Batt. N.Yorks. Regt. for temporary duty. Capt Pope proceeded on leave to England. Medical examination held on troops of + Area Commandant, 2. 62nd Div. Salvage Coy, 3. Musketry Officer.	
"	-27			
"	-28		Nothing to report.	
"	-29		Capt Mackenzie returned to duty from Paris. Plage. A.D.M.S. visited the Camp. Medical Examination held on personnel of 132 Army hospital.	
"	-30		Nothing to report.	
"	-31		Nothing to report.	

LIEUT-COL., R.A.M.C. (T)
2/1st W.R. FIELD AMBULANCE
ROYAL ARMY MEDICAL CORPS (T.)

Army Form C. 2118.

WAR DIARY
or
INTELLIGENCE SUMMARY.

(Erase heading not required.)

ORIGINAL

— Confidential —

WAR DIARY
— of —

2/1st West Riding Field Ambce

From 1st Sept 1917 To 30th Sept 1917

(Volume IX)

COMMITTEE FOR THE
MEDICAL HISTORY OF THE WAR
Date — 5 NOV. 1917

Army Form C. 2118.

WAR DIARY
or
INTELLIGENCE SUMMARY.
(Erase heading not required.)

Instructions regarding War Diaries and Intelligence Summaries are contained in F. S. Regs., Part II. and the Staff Manual respectively. Title pages will be prepared in manuscript.

Place	Date	Hour	Summary of Events and Information	Remarks and references to Appendices
In the field	1/9/17		Capt. L.A. MacKenzie & party relieved Capt. A.W.Robinson and party at the A.D.S. and forward area. Limited A.D.M.S. Personnel commenced erecting hutments for new Camp.	
	2/9/17		One N.C.O. & five men proceeded to Rest Camp, St Valery. A similar number returned from Rest Camp.	
	3/9/17		Medical examination of two men 5/7 K Seaforth Highlanders. A.D.M.S. visited the Camp.	
	4/9/17		Invited A.D.M.S. and Division re Stores at Gauchaupré.	
	5/9/17		Nothing to report.	
	6/9/17		Capt. A.W.Robinson relieved Capt. H.D. Bickers who was acting temporarily as M.O./c 7/6 W.Yorks Regt. Capt. Proctor returned to the M.D.S.-Sick. Ten P.B. men arrived to replace ten A.S.C. men (officers batmen)	
	7/9/17		Ten A.S.C. men (officers batmen) left for H.T. & S. Depot Havre. Capt. J.H.Blackburn relieved Capt. L.A. MacKenzie at the A.D.S.	A.D.M.S. M5947 of 27/8/17

A5834 Wt. W4973/M687 750,000 8/16 D. D. & L. Ltd. Forms/C.2118/13.

Army Form C. 2118.

WAR DIARY
or
INTELLIGENCE SUMMARY.
(Erase heading not required.)

Instructions regarding War Diaries and Intelligence Summaries are contained in F. S. Regs., Part II. and the Staff Manual respectively. Title pages will be prepared in manuscript.

Place	Date	Hour	Summary of Events and Information	Remarks and references to Appendices
In the field	8/9/17		Nothing to report.	
	9/9/17		A.D.M.S. 62nd Division conducted D.D.M.S. VI Corps over the Camp & inspected Hospital.	
	10/9/17		Capt. C.S. Brown proceeded to England on leave.	
	11/9/17		Accompanied A.D.M.S. to Lanchamps	
	12/9/17		Nothing to report	
	13/9/17		Nothing to report	
	14/9/17		Capt. H.D. Dickles went to A.D.S. for duty. Capt. A.W. Robinson returned from 2/6th Batt. N. Yorks. Regt.	
	15/9/17		Capt. H.R. Pope commenced a four days Course at the Div. Gas School, Yauconil.	A.D.M.S. M/6346 of 14/9/17
	16/9/17		Nothing to report.	

Army Form C. 2118.

WAR DIARY
or
INTELLIGENCE SUMMARY.
(Erase heading not required.)

Place	Date	Hour	Summary of Events and Information	Remarks and references to Appendices
Lichfield	17/9/17		Nothing to report	
	18/9/17		Capt. A.W.Robinson recommenced for M.C. by O.C. 25th Bath. Works Regt.	
	19/9/17		Capt. A.G.Pope terminated Course at Dweller School Farnworth 1st Kent. W.R.Horse. O.S.M.C. reported to this Unit for duty.	
	20/9/17		Capt. W.S.Robinson took up temporary duty at H.Q.E. 25th Bath. W.Works Regt. pending return of Capt. C.S.Brown on leave. Capt. C.S.Brown struck off the strength of this Unit & detailed as Adjut. 25th Bath. W.Works Regt.	Comm. M/542/30 of 19/9/17
	21/9/17		Proceeded to England on leave Capt. H.B.Pope M.C. During my absence Capt. L.A.Mackenzie M.C. proceeded to A.D.M.S. office for temporary duty	
	22/9/17		A.D.M.S. inspected Hospital, Stables & Camp.	A.D.S.

Army Form C. 2118.

WAR DIARY
or
INTELLIGENCE SUMMARY.
(Erase heading not required.)

Instructions regarding War Diaries and Intelligence Summaries are contained in F. S. Regs., Part II. and the Staff Manual respectively. Title pages will be prepared in manuscript.

Place	Date	Hour	Summary of Events and Information	Remarks and references to Appendices
In the field	23/9/17		Nothing to report.	D.S.O.
"	24/9/17		Capt. C.C. Brown returned from leave & took up duties as M.O. 9th Battn. W.Yorks Regt., relieving Capt. H.W. Robinson who was acting temporarily.	D.S.O.
"	25/9/17		Capt. N.D. Pickles proceeded to 7/8th Battn. W.Yorks Regt. to act as M.O. during Capt. D.L. Ball's absence on leave.	D.S.O.
"	26/9/17		Nothing to report.	D.S.O.
"	27/9/17		Visited the forward area to investigate route of evacuation during the coming month.	D.S.O.
"	28/9/17		Nothing to report.	D.S.O.
"	29/9/17		Nothing to report.	D.S.O.
"	30/9/17		Nothing to report.	D.S.O.

for Captain, R.A.M.C. (T.D.)
O.C. 2/1st W.R. FIELD AMBULANCE
ROYAL ARMY MEDICAL CORPS (T.F.)

WAR DIARY
or
INTELLIGENCE SUMMARY.

Army Form C. 2118.

— Confidential —

WAR DIARY
of
2/1st West Riding Field Ambulance

From 1-10-17 To 31-10-17.

Volume X

ORIGINAL

COMMITTEE FOR THE
MEDICAL HISTORY OF THE WAR
Date — 8 DEC. 1917

WAR DIARY
or
INTELLIGENCE SUMMARY.
(Erase heading not required.)

Army Form C. 2118.

Instructions regarding War Diaries and Intelligence Summaries are contained in F. S. Regs., Part II. and the Staff Manual respectively. Title pages will be prepared in manuscript.

Place	Date	Hour	Summary of Events and Information	Remarks and references to Appendices
Indefield	1/10/17		Two Officers of U.S.M.C arrived for instruction for one week.	ADMS No. 6559 dated 30/9/17
"	2/10/17		Capt. C.S. Brown returned from 1/4 West Riding Regt. (sick) Capt. Robinson relieved temporarily. Consultation U.S.M.C Officers over the Forward Area - R.A.P's, A.D.S & Relay Posts	AM
"	3/10/17		Returned from leave today	AK
"	4/10/17		Nothing to report.	AK
"	5/10/17		ADMS visited the Camp.	AK
"	6/10/17		Lieut Howse U.S.M.C proceeded to 2/7 West Riding Regt to act temporarily as Medical Officer	AK
"	7/10/17		Two U.S.M.C Officers proceeded to No. 45 C.C.S. for instruction	ADMS H. No 6679 dated 30/9/17
"	8/10/17		Instructions received to move to new Camp at Baroche	RAMC Brev DO No 18 Copy No 13

Army Form C. 2118.

WAR DIARY
or
INTELLIGENCE SUMMARY.
(Erase heading not required.)

Instructions regarding War Diaries and Intelligence Summaries are contained in F. S. Regs., Part II. and the Staff Manual respectively. Title pages will be prepared in manuscript.

Place	Date	Hour	Summary of Events and Information	Remarks and references to Appendices
Inkerfield	9/10/17		Located site of New Camp at Baraste. One N.C.O. & Energy 113th Field Amb. arrived at M.D.S. Proceeded to A.D.S. (Dugong Part). Capt. E. Brown evacuated to No 49 C.C.S.	M.S/6228 dated 8/10/17
"	10/10/17		Advance party of One Officer & 28 other ranks proceeded to New Camp at Baraste. One Officer & 40 other ranks arrived from 7th Field Amb. and proceeded to A.D.S. to learn the line.	
"	11/10/17		Capt. A. Blackburn and party returned to M.D.S. having been relieved by 7th Field Ambulance. O.O.C. Commanded the Camp.	
"	12/10/17		The Ambulance moved to New Camp at Baraste. Capt. Blackburn proceeded on leave to England.	
"	13/10/17		Arranged for Collection of Brigade sick daily	
"	14/10/17		D.D.M.S. IV Corps visited the Camp. Lieut. Home returned to Unit for duty from 2/4th W. Riding Regt.	

Army Form C. 2118.

WAR DIARY
or
INTELLIGENCE SUMMARY.
(Erase heading not required.)

Instructions regarding War Diaries and Intelligence Summaries are contained in F.S. Regs., Part II. and the Staff Manual respectively. Title pages will be prepared in manuscript.

Place	Date	Hour	Summary of Events and Information	Remarks and references to Appendices
Inkpield	15/15/17		A.D.M.S. provided the Camp.	
	16/15/17		Nothing to report.	
	17/15/17		Nothing to report.	
	18/15/17		A.D.M.S. visited the Camp.	
	19/15/17		Lieut. Q.M. B. Glanvar proceeded on leave to England.	
	20/15/17		Capt. A.D. Pickles returned to this Unit for duty from 2/8th West Yorks Regt.	
	21/15/17		Nothing to report.	
	22/15/17		D.D.M.S. IV Corps visited the Camp.	
	23/15/17		Capt. K.A. Mackenzie M.C. proceeded on leave to England.	
	24/15/17		Capt. J.S. Blackburn returned from leave.	

Army Form C. 2118.

WAR DIARY
or
INTELLIGENCE SUMMARY.
(Erase heading not required.)

Place	Date	Hour	Summary of Events and Information	Remarks and references to Appendices
Infequil	25/10/17		Nothing to report.	
"	26/10/17		Nothing to report.	
"	27/10/17		Orders received to move to Barly Area on the 28th inst. This Unit to march out at 10.0 a.m. & billet at Gomiecourt.	Absent from 25.27/10/17 1st & 2nd Sept Bar Order No 48 of 27/10/17.
"	28/10/17		The Ambulance moved to Gomiecourt; leaving rear-party of One Officer & 5 other ranks at Barastre.	
"	29/10/17		The Ambulance left Gomiecourt and arrived at New Site, Barly at 6.0 p.m.	
"	30/10/17		Arrangements made for Collection of Brigade Sick.	
"	31/10/17		Lieut & Q.M. B. F. Gibson returned from leave. Three other ranks returned from St. Valery Rest Camp. Capt. Fortesque M.C. R.A.M.C. T. reported to this Unit.	

Lieut.-Col., R.A.M.C. (T)
2/1th W.R. FIELD AMBULANCE

"MEDICAL"

Army Form C. 2118.

WAR DIARY
or
INTELLIGENCE SUMMARY.
(Erase heading not required.)

Summary of Events and Information

Confidential.

ORIGINAL.

WAR DIARY
of
2/1st West Riding Field Amb=

Period:- Nov 1st To Nov 30th

Volume XI

COMMITTEE FOR THE
MEDICAL HISTORY OF THE WAR
Date   17 JAN 1918

MEDICAL.

Army Form C. 2118.

WAR DIARY
or
INTELLIGENCE SUMMARY.
(Erase heading not required.)

Instructions regarding War Diaries and Intelligence Summaries are contained in F.S. Regs., Part II. and the Staff Manual respectively. Title pages will be prepared in manuscript.

Place	Date	Hour	Summary of Events and Information	Remarks and references to Appendices
In the field	1/11/17		Nothing to report.	
"	2/11/17		ADMS. XVII Corps ADMS. 63rd Division visited the Camp.	
"	3/11/17		Capt. McRobinson struck off the strength of the Unit. Capt. A. Mackenzie returned from leave.	ADMS Order No. 72/6
"	4/11/17		Nothing to report.	
"	5/11/17		Brigade Order No.50 received instructing Stores to be sent to Bernaville on the 6th inst & that the Unit move on the 7th to mat	
"	6/11/17		Instructions re move contained in Bde Order No.50 cancelled.	
"	7/11/17		Nothing to report.	
"	8/11/17		Nothing to report.	

WAR DIARY
or
INTELLIGENCE SUMMARY.

(Erase heading not required.)

Army Form C. 2118.

Place	Date	Hour	Summary of Events and Information	Remarks and references to Appendices
In the field	9/11/17		Located as M.S. 62nd Division.	A2
	10/11/17		Nothing to report.	A2
	11/11/17		Nothing to report.	A2
	12/11/17		Instructions received for Unit to proceed to Corcelles-le-Comte. The Ambulance left Barly at 6.0 pm.	A2
	13/11/17		The Unit arrived at Corcelles-le-Comte at 7.45am. Left for Parade at 8.0 pm. Night very dark.	A2
	14/11/17		The Unit arrived at Parade 3.0 am.	A2
	15/11/17		The Unit camped at Parade for the day.	A2
	16/11/17		The Ambulance left Parade at 5.0 pm & arrived at Bertincourt at 7.0 pm.	A2

WAR DIARY
or
INTELLIGENCE SUMMARY.
(Erase heading not required.)

Army Form C. 2118.

Place	Date	Hour	Summary of Events and Information	Remarks and references to Appendices
Lillers	17/10/17		One Bearer Sub-division ready to move at short notice.	Card Divn RAMC Orders No 21. Sept 17
	18/10/17		A.D.M.S. visited the Camp.	
	19/10/17		Capt. K.A. Mackenzie 9th Lieut. W.H. Horne proceeded to No 21 C.C.S. for temporary duty. Four Clerks sent to No 21 CCS for temporary duty. Two officers & 38 other Ranks proceeded to 73 L.R.F. Ambce to duty in the forward area. Mail came forward area	Nº 1559 instructions of same Nº 1511
	20/10/17		One Officer 1/c of One Bearer Sub Division sent to 73 LRF Ambce for duty 20/94. One Officer 14 of One Bearer Sub-division to the line. One sent Sub-division sent to 2/3 LRF Ambce for duty in the line. Capt H.S. Wayli awaiting to C.C.S.	20/94.
	21/10/17		All available transport sent to 73 LRF Ambce. A.D.S. established at Van Caud	20/94
	22/10/17		Three Bearer Squads sent to Capt Pictise at Kernus, Crucifix ADS at Hernies. Motor transport sent to 73/LRF Ambce.	20/94

WAR DIARY
or
INTELLIGENCE SUMMARY.
(Erase heading not required.)

Army Form C. 2118.

Place	Date	Hour	Summary of Events and Information	Remarks and references to Appendices
[illegible]	22/11/17		Nothing to report	[initials]
	23/11/17		All personnel returned to Headquarters from the forward area.	[initials]
	25/11/17		The Unit moved to Lecanere. Bearer Sub-divisions & one Tent-Sub-division sent to 73 W.R.Y. Ambce for duty in the forward area.	Battn Order No 22 [initials]
	26/11/17		One Bearer Sub-division sent to 73 W.R.Y. Ambce for duty in the line. Four men of this Unit wounded. Horse Ambulance sent to 73 W.R.Y. Ambce to assist in evacuation of wounded.	[initials]
	27/11/17		Invited A.D.S. Barincourt.	[initials]
	28/11/17		All available transport carrying in evacuation of wounded.	[initials]
	29/11/17		Proceeded to A.D.S. Barincourt.	[initials]

Army Form C. 2118.

WAR DIARY
or
INTELLIGENCE SUMMARY.
(Erase heading not required.)

Place	Date	Hour	Summary of Events and Information	Remarks and references to Appendices
Inkerville	30/4/17		Returned from ADS. Haronn Court. The Unit moved off at noon to new Camp at Dicaucto. Camp at Dicaucto heavily shelled prior to departure & road from Dicaucto to Metz constantly shelled along the whole distance. Fifteen Casualties picked up by Moto Transport of the Unit and taken to No 2 CCS & Camp at Dicaucto, under fire intermittently. Moto Ambulances sent to OC MAC Dicaucto to assist in evacuation.	Brigadier RAMC Order No 23.

J. W. Hodes
Lieut Col RAMC (T)
71. W. R. Field Amber.

COMMITTEE FOR THE
MEDICAL HISTORY OF THE WAR

Date -1 FEB. 1918

WAR DIARY
or
INTELLIGENCE SUMMARY.

ORIGINAL

Army Form C. 2118.

"MEDICAL"

Confidential

WAR DIARY
— of —
2/1st West Riding Field Ambulance

Period 1st – 31st Decr/17.

Volume XII

"MEDICAL"

No. Army Form C.2118.
Date...........

2/1 W.R. FIELD AMBULANCE
R.A.M.C. (T.F.)

WAR DIARY
or
INTELLIGENCE SUMMARY.
(Erase heading not required.)

Instructions regarding War Diaries and Intelligence Summaries are contained in F. S. Regs., Part II. and the Staff Manual respectively. Title pages will be prepared in manuscript.

Place	Date	Hour	Summary of Events and Information	Remarks and references to Appendices
Inkafield	1/3/17	—	Nothing to report	AZ
"	2/3/17	—	Vicinity of Camp Shelled. No casualties in Unit.	AZ
"	3/3/17		Vicinity of Camp Shelled. No casualties in Unit. Orders received for Unit to move to Gnocourt. 18th Bde Orders on the 4th inst. No. 65.	AZ
"	4/3/17		Entrained at Zeincourt. Transport moved by road. Stores arrived. Arrived 3.0 am. Billeted in Hopulados Weillards.	AZ
"	5/3/17		Orders received to move under 18 FA Bd Orders to Savy Berlette.	AZ
"	6/3/17		Unit moved by road to Savy-Berlette. Arrived 4.0 pm.	AZ
"	7/3/17		Nothing to report	AZ
"	8/3/17		Orders received for Unit to move to Roores Area	AZ
"	9/3/17		Nothing to report	AZ

WAR DIARY
or
INTELLIGENCE SUMMARY.
(Erase heading not required.)

Army Form C. 2118.

Instructions regarding War Diaries and Intelligence Summaries are contained in F. S. Regs., Part II. and the Staff Manual respectively. Title pages will be prepared in manuscript.

Place	Date	Hour	Summary of Events and Information	Remarks and references to Appendices
Lillefield	10/9/17		Nothing to report	H
"	11/9/17		Enemy Aeroplane passed overhead twice 6.30pm. Bombs dropped some considerable distance away	H
"	12/9/17		1st Lieut. R. Howe, MRC, USA struck off the strength of this Unit. Posted to R.A.M.C. Base D.A.C.	Army Lists posted H/2
"	13/9/17		Preparations for move to Annezin on the 14th inst. under 186th Infantry Brigade Orders	Bombdown order No. 69 copy 17 H/2
"	14/9/17		Unit moved to ANNEZIN. Billeted in School. Arrangements made to take all Divisional sick	186th Bde arrangements 26/6 copy 2 and Annexures H/2
"	15/9/17		Sergt. Blakebrough recommended for Meritorious Service Medal. Pte Odgers & Summerscales awarded the Military Medal	SSDO 10/15 dated 15/9/17 H/2
"	16/9/17		Nothing to report	
"	17/9/17		Orders received for Unit to move to HOUDELIN under 186th Infantry Bde Orders - on the 19th inst.	186th Inf Bde Orders No. H/2

WAR DIARY
or
INTELLIGENCE SUMMARY.
(Erase heading not required.)

Army Form C. 2118.

Instructions regarding War Diaries and Intelligence Summaries are contained in F. S. Regs., Part II. and the Staff Manual respectively. Title pages will be prepared in manuscript.

Place	Date	Hour	Summary of Events and Information	Remarks and references to Appendices
Inchicourt	18/9/17		Unit moved to HOUVELIN. Roads very dusty for horse transport to proceed. Arrived destination at 5.35pm	
	19/9/17		Arrangements made to collect Brigade Sick. Instructions received re inspection of transport	18" Divn M.O. MH/119
	20/9/17		Nothing to report	
	21/9/17		Weather Conditions very severe - Traffic held up on account of snow drifts. Inspection of horse transport cancelled	18" Divn M.O. transport
	22/9/17		Weather Conditions severe. Roads cleared of snow	
	23/9/17		Capt Robinson R.M.C.(T) proceeded to 1/4 K.O.Y.L.I. to act temporarily on C.O.M.S. Letter M.O.'s Batn during absence of Capt Mud - on leave.	18" Divn M.O. 82 dn 24/9/17
	24/9/17		Nothing to report	
	25/9/17		Xmas Day. Wire received "Adopt thaw precautions"	

WAR DIARY
or
INTELLIGENCE SUMMARY.

(Erase heading not required.)

Army Form C. 2118.

Instructions regarding War Diaries and Intelligence Summaries are contained in F.S. Regs., Part II. and the Staff Manual respectively. Title pages will be prepared in manuscript.

Place	Date	Hour	Summary of Events and Information	Remarks and references to Appendices
Inkipilos	26/10/17		Wire received "Resume Normal traffic"	
	27/10/17		Nothing to report	
	28/10/17		Nothing to report	
	29/10/17		Weather Conditions again very severe. Heavy snow on roads on account of snow drifts.	
	30/10/17		Nothing to report	
	31/10/17		Capt Blackburn J.N. R.M.S.(T) & Capt Buckles, H.D. (R.A.M.C.(T) Awarded the Military Cross for gallantry during operation commencing 30/10/17	G.R.O./1083 dated 31/10/17

Signed,
LIEUT-COL, R.A.M.C. (T)
2/1st W.R. FIELD AMBULANCE
ROYAL ARMY MEDICAL CORPS (T.F.)

"MEDICAL"

Army Form C. 2118.

ORIGINAL

WAR DIARY
or
INTELLIGENCE SUMMARY.
(Erase heading not required.)

Summary of Events and Information

Instructions regarding War Diaries and Intelligence Summaries are contained in F.S. Regs., Part II. and the Staff Manual respectively. Title pages will be prepared in manuscript.

Place	Date	Hour

COMMITTEE FOR THE
MEDICAL HISTORY OF THE WAR
Date -4 MAR 1918

— Confidential —

WAR DIARY
— of —

2/1st West Riding Field Ambce

Period :- Jany 1st/18 to Jany 31st/18

Volume XIII

"MEDICAL"

Army Form C. 2118.

ORIGINAL

WAR DIARY
or
INTELLIGENCE SUMMARY.
(Erase heading not required.)

Instructions regarding War Diaries and Intelligence Summaries are contained in F.S. Regs., Part II. and the Staff Manual respectively. Title pages will be prepared in manuscript.

Place	Date	Hour	Summary of Events and Information	Remarks and references to Appendices
In the Field	1/1/18		Capt L. Mackenzie to ADMS office for temporary duty as D.A.D.M.S.	ADMS letter no 3240
	2/1/18		Nothing to report	
	3/1/18		Orders received for Unit to move to Cambligneul on the 5th & St Catherine on the 6th & take over the Main Dressing Station there	62nd Divn RAMC Order no 9
	4/1/18		Preparations for move - Advance party sent to St Catherine	
	5/1/18		Unit moved off at 10.0 a.m. Arrived at Cambligneul at 2.0 pm & billeted for the night. Accommodation - good.	-do-
	6/1/18		Unit moved off from Cambligneul at 10.0 a.m. and arrived at St Catherine at 1.45 p.m. Took over from outgoing Field Ambulance at 7.0 p.m.	-do-
	7/1/18		Outgoing Field Ambulance marched off at 9.0 a.m.	
	8/1/18		Nothing to report	

T2134. Wt. W708—776. 500000. 4/15. Sir J.C. & S.

'Army Form C. 2118.

Original

WAR DIARY
or
INTELLIGENCE SUMMARY.
(Erase heading not required.)

Instructions regarding War Diaries and Intelligence Summaries are contained in F. S. Regs., Part II. and the Staff Manual respectively. Title pages will be prepared in manuscript.

Place	Date	Hour	Summary of Events and Information	Remarks and references to Appendices
In the field	9/1/18		ADMS 62nd Division inspected the Main Dressing Station	H
	10/1/18		Nothing to report.	H
	11/1/18		Capt A.S. Robinson returned to Unit	H
	12/1/18		Capt A.S. Robinson proceeded on leave to England. Capt H.D. Pickles proceeded to 2/4th Bn. Works Regt for temporary duty as Medical Officer. AFW3353	H
	13/1/18		Nothing to report.	H
	14/1/18		Nothing to report.	H
	15/1/18		Nothing to report.	H
	16/1/18		ADMS visited the M.D.S.	H

T2134. Wt. W708—776. 500000. 4/15. Sir J. C. & S.

Army Form C. 2118.

Original

WAR DIARY
or
INTELLIGENCE SUMMARY.
(Erase heading not required.)

Instructions regarding War Diaries and Intelligence Summaries are contained in F. S. Regs., Part II. and the Staff Manual respectively. Title pages will be prepared in manuscript.

Place	Date	Hour	Summary of Events and Information	Remarks and references to Appendices
In the field	17/1/18		Capt. K.A. Mackenzie returned to Unit from ADMS Office.	H
	18/1/18		Working Party sent to 62nd D.H.Q.	H
	19/1/18		ADMS visited the M.D.S	H
	20/1/18		Working Party sent to West Rochincourt Camp	H
	21/1/18		Nothing to report.	H
	22/1/18		Attended meeting at Office of ADMS 62nd Division	H
	23/1/18		1 Officer & 1 N.C.O. proceeded to First Army R.A.M.C School of Instruction.	ADMS Instr. negs H
	24/1/18		Medical Officer detailed to attend to sick of 62nd Div R.E & 62nd Div Train A.S.C.	ADMS Instr negs H

T2134. Wt. W708—776. 500000. 4/15. Sir J. C. & S.

Army Form C. 2118.

Original

WAR DIARY
or
INTELLIGENCE SUMMARY.
(Erase heading not required.)

Instructions regarding War Diaries and Intelligence Summaries are contained in F.S. Regs., Part II. and the Staff Manual respectively. Title pages will be prepared in manuscript.

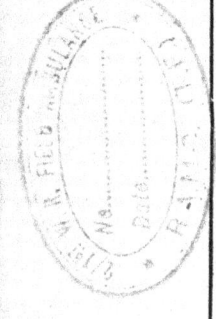

Place	Date	Hour	Summary of Events and Information	Remarks and references to Appendices
In the field	25/1/18		Medical Inspection of personnel of 62nd D.I.C	Copies letter M.937/9/4
	26/1/18		Medical Inspection of personnel of 62nd D.I.C Completed	-do- 4/-
	27/1/18		Capt A.Pope detailed for duty with 2/Brd. W.R. Field Amber in exchange for Capt - Sharard, who reported to this Unit for temporary duty today	4/-
	28/1/18		Capt. A.B. Robinson returned from leave.	4/-
	29/1/18		G.O.C. Division inspected the M.D.S and transport of the Unit. Capt H.Robinson proceeded to 2/6th W.Yorks Regt for temporary duty as Medical Officer.	Copy letter M.9025 4/-
	30/1/18		Capt J.Pickles returned to Unit from 2/9th Bn. W.Yorks Regt. 10 Welsh duty men from 2/5, 2/6 + 2/8 West Yorks Regts reported to this Unit for duty were taken on the strength.	Copies letter M.9039 4/-
	31/1/18		Nothing to report.	4/-

Walter Foster
LIEUT.-COL., R.A.M.C. (T)
2/1st W.R. FIELD AMBULANCE
ROYAL ARMY MEDICAL CORPS (T.F.)

Plan of the D.S. at St Catherine attached 4 feet with Plane.

WAR DIARY
or
INTELLIGENCE SUMMARY.
(Erase heading not required.)

— Confidential —

WAR DIARY
of

2/1st West Riding Field Amb ce

Period 1st to 28th February 1918.

Volume XIV

WAR DIARY
or
INTELLIGENCE SUMMARY.
(Erase heading not required.)

Instructions regarding War Diaries and Intelligence Summaries are contained in F.S. Regs., Part II. and the Staff Manual respectively. Title pages will be prepared in manuscript.

Army Form C. 2118
1/7th E.LAN. R. FIELD AMBULANCE
R.A.M.C. (T.F.)
MEDICAL
ORIGINAL

Place	Date	Hour	Summary of Events and Information	Remarks and references to Appendices
St. Catherine	1-2-18		A.D.M.S. visited Main Dressing Station	L.Q. Welsh
Shed 57	2-2-18		Nothing to report	L.G. Welsh
Q.15.a.7.5.	3-2-18		R.D.M.S. inspected M.D.S.	Welsh
"	4-2-18		Nothing to report	L.Q. Welsh
"	5-2-18		Nothing to report	L.Q. Welsh
"	6-2-18		Capt. Pickler & N.C.O. sent to Army R.A.M.C. school. Capt. Robinson sent to 5th N.R. Regt. as temp. M.O.	ADMS 6622 Welsh
"	7-2-18		Conference at offices of D.D.M.S. XIII Corps - O.C. 2/3 L'don Fd Amb re visit M.D.S. Arrangements completed for relief	9222 Welsh
"	8-2-18		Advance party from 2/3 L'don Fd Ambce consisting of 1 Sub. Officer arrived at M.D.S.	Welsh
"	9-2-18		M.D.S. handed over to incoming unit at 7 p.m. Advance party sent therein to take over fr. 2/3 L'don Fd Ambce	Welsh
Herinnes	10-2-18		Ambce marched off at 10 a.m. - arrived Herinnes 3 p.m. billets good - plans attached. Arrangements made for daily collection of sick.	Welsh
Shed 366				
P.28.a.7.8.	11-2-18		Received 187th Inf. Bde. Order (B.M.H. #46/2) re entraining	Welsh
"	12-2-18		Received 187th Inf. Bde. Order (B.M.H. #49/2) re entraining	Welsh
"	13-2-18		Training of Fd Ambce according to programme - repair of billets - erection of horse stand dumps & cook house begun.	Welsh
"	14-2-18		Medical exam of 6/7th A.S.C. personnel who were all examined in four.	Welsh
"	15-2-18		Lecture on "Cleanliness of Sanitation with sp. reference to lice & dust given to Officers & N.C.O.s 187 Bde Concurrent	ADMS Letter M944 Welsh

WAR DIARY or INTELLIGENCE SUMMARY

Army Form C. 2118

Instructions regarding War Diaries and Intelligence Summaries are contained in F. S. Regs., Part II. and the Staff Manual respectively. Title pages will be prepared in manuscript.

Place	Date	Hour	Summary of Events and Information	Remarks and references to Appendices
Herrin Shed 36.t. P.28 a.7-5.	20-2-18		Capt. Mackenzie sent as temp. M.O. to 2/5 N. York Rgt.	Lauer
	22-2-18		Lecture given at Hqrs viva voci on Cleanliness & Sanitation to Officers & NCOs 187th Inf. Bde.	ADMS Etc. M.9 + 77
"			Capt. Robinson relieved Capt. Mackenzie as temp. M.O. to 2/5 R.m.F. York Rgt.	Lauer
"	26-2-18		62nd Divisional Horse Show. Two prizes awarded to 2/1st W.R. Fd. Amb. for best Field Ambulance Wagon.	Lauer
"			62nd Div. R.A.M.C. Orders No. 31 receives. Visited Fd. Amb's site at Mond St Eloi tunnels encampments for taking over on 28th inst.	Lauer
"	27-2-18		Advance party of Capt. Potts & one Fd Sub division sent to hunt St Eloi. Advance party 3rd W. Amb. arrived	L.G.H.R.
Mond St Eloi Sheet 51C. F.8.c.g.5.	28-2-18		Ambulance moved to Mond St Eloi - marched H.Q. 9-30 a.m. arrive 10. a.m. accomodation good.	Lauer

LIEUT.-COL.

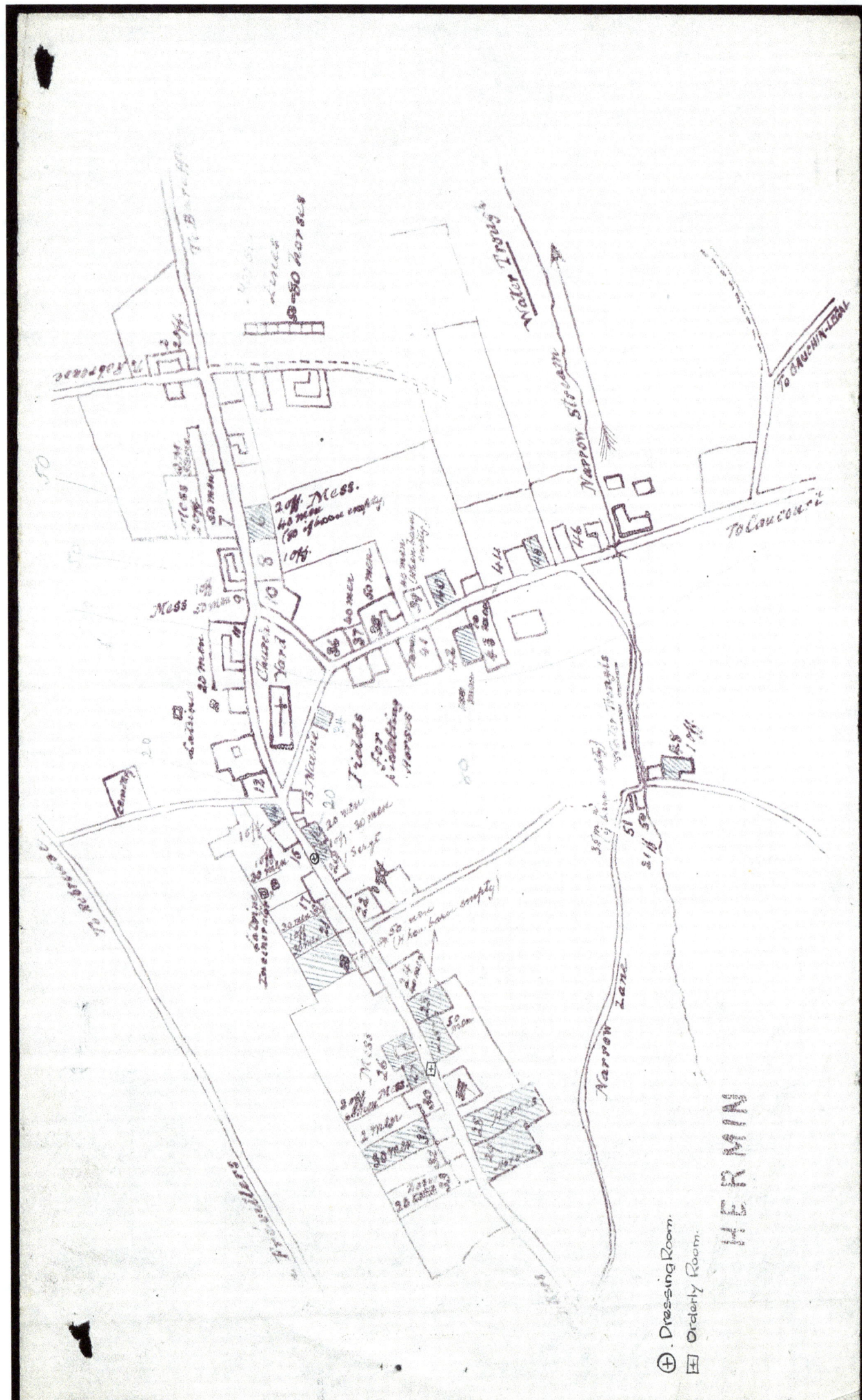

2/1 W. R. FIELD AMBULANCE
Army Form C. 2118.
No.................
Date.................
R.A.M.C. (T.F.)

WAR DIARY
or
INTELLIGENCE SUMMARY.
(Erase heading not required.)

Instructions regarding War Diaries and Intelligence Summaries are contained in F. S. Regs., Part II. and the Staff Manual respectively. Title pages will be prepared in manuscript.

Place	Date	Hour	Summary of Events and Information	Remarks and references to Appendices

T2134. Wt. W708—776. 500000. 4/15. Sir J. C. & S.

WAR DIARY
or
INTELLIGENCE SUMMARY.

Confidential.

WAR DIARY
of
2/1st West Riding Fld Amb'ce

Period 1st March/18 to 31st March/18

Volume XIV

140/2849

COMMITTEE FOR THE
MEDICAL HISTORY OF THE WAR
Date 12 MAY 1918

ORIGINAL

March 1918

WAR DIARY
or
INTELLIGENCE SUMMARY.

(Erase heading not required.)

Army Form C. 2118
W.R. FIELD AMBULANCE
R.A.M.C. (T.F.)

Instructions regarding War Diaries and Intelligence Summaries are contained in F.S. Regs., Part II. and the Staff Manual respectively. Title pages will be prepared in manuscript.

— ORIGINAL —

Place	Date	Hour	Summary of Events and Information	Remarks and references to Appendices
MONT-ST-ELOI 51c F8 d.3.3.	1918 MAR 1		Local Sick Parade	
	2		Advance party of 10 Officers + 39 O.R. proceeded to Aubigny to take over XIII C.R.S. + Officers' R.S.	
AUBIGNY G12. C.R.S. E1.c.5.4 O.R.S.D.12.b.5.8	3		Advance party took over XIII C.R.S. + O.R.S. as from 12 noon this day	
	4		Unit moved to XIII C.R.S.	
	5		New encampment begun. Horse lines ready — 1/3rd S/Arm. 3/4th W.J.A. reported to unit this day	
	6		1/2nd S/Arm. 2/3rd R.J.A. relieved 1/2nd S/Arm. 2/3rd R.J.A.	
	7		A.M.S. 1st Army inspected C.R.S.	
	8		Inspector of Catering visited C.R.S.	
	15		Enemy aeroplanes bombed the vicinity shortly after 8 P.M.	
	17		Two M.O.s (M.O.R.E., U.S.A.) reported for duty with this Field Ambulance	
	18		Stables dismantled. Fresh room for 17 C.C.S.	
	19		Lecture to Staff on new S.B. Gun wound	
	20		1 Officer sent to Conference of Wounded Education Officers — 10 Officers 2/3rd R.F.A. rejoined this unit	
	22		Instructions issued to move to BERNEVILLE on 25th	
			Sent two vehicle to long the Army S.I. at XIII C.R.S.	
	24		Preparations made for handing over C.R.S. Advance party 1/2/3 London Fd Ambce arrived	

WAR DIARY
or
INTELLIGENCE SUMMARY.
(Erase heading not required.)

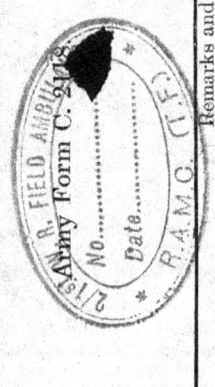

Army Form C. 2118

Instructions regarding War Diaries and Intelligence Summaries are contained in F.S. Regs., Part II. and the Staff Manual respectively. Title pages will be prepared in manuscript.

ORIGINAL

Place	Date	Hour	Summary of Events and Information	Remarks and references to Appendices
AUBIGNY 51C	1918 MAR			
C.R.S. E.1.C.5.4 O.R.S. D.12.6.5.8	24th		C.R.S. handed over at 6p.m. — Destination for unit altered to ARRAS.	Order by 2nd RAMC pty 35
ARRAS	25		Unit marched to ARRAS - left 10p.m. arrived 6p.m. — Instructions received there to move to BUCQUOY as soon as possible. — Unit moved from ARRAS at 9 p.m.	187 Bde wire BM ½ 54/2 AM
BIENVILLERS	26		Unit arrived BIENVILLERS at 6.40 a.m. Shortly afterwards reading orders - Unit moved to HUMBERCAMPS 1.30 p.m.	AM
HUMBERCAMPS	27		On arrival 2 Officers & 60 Bearers sent to help wd A.D.S. HANNESCAMPS & 187 B.H.2. GOMMECOURT. On 2 Lt & 2 NCO's & 36 Junmen were pulled off performing burial duty 12 am — MDS opened at HUMBERCAMPS 8 p.m. took over M.D.S. HUMBERCAMPS from o/c N.T.Andrea at 1 p.m.	AM AM
			4 Officers at LA CAUCHIE at 8 p.m. - 24 bearers sent to A.D.S. HANNESCAMPS	AM
LA CAUCHIE 51C V.7.6.7.2	28		Bearers atturnd in forward area - 411 cases through M.D.S.	AM
	29		446 cases through M.D.S.	AM
	30		Enemy shelled vicinity with shrapnel - 275 cases through M.D.S.	AM
	31		Relief parts send to forward area - 192 cases through M.D.S. Instructions received for two coys 63rd Bn RAMC to move to HENU on 2nd April. Advance party to be sent to take over billets on 1st April	AM 36 ADMS Div M.2.6

signature

LIEUT.-COL., R.A.M.C. (T)
2/1ST W.R. FIELD AMBULANCE.

WAR DIARY
or
INTELLIGENCE SUMMARY.

(Erase heading not required.)

Instructions regarding War Diaries and Intelligence Summaries are contained in F.S. Regs., Part II. and the Staff Manual respectively. Title pages will be prepared in manuscript.

1st/W. Riding Field Ambulance
R.A.M.C. (T.F.)

Place	Date	Hour	Summary of Events and Information	Remarks and references to Appendices

T2134. Wt. W708—776. 500000. 4/15. Sir J. C. & S.

Chart showing no of Cases remaining in C.R.S. at 2 p.m & 6 p.m daily.

Chart showing No of cases remaining in CRS at 2pm & 6pm daily.

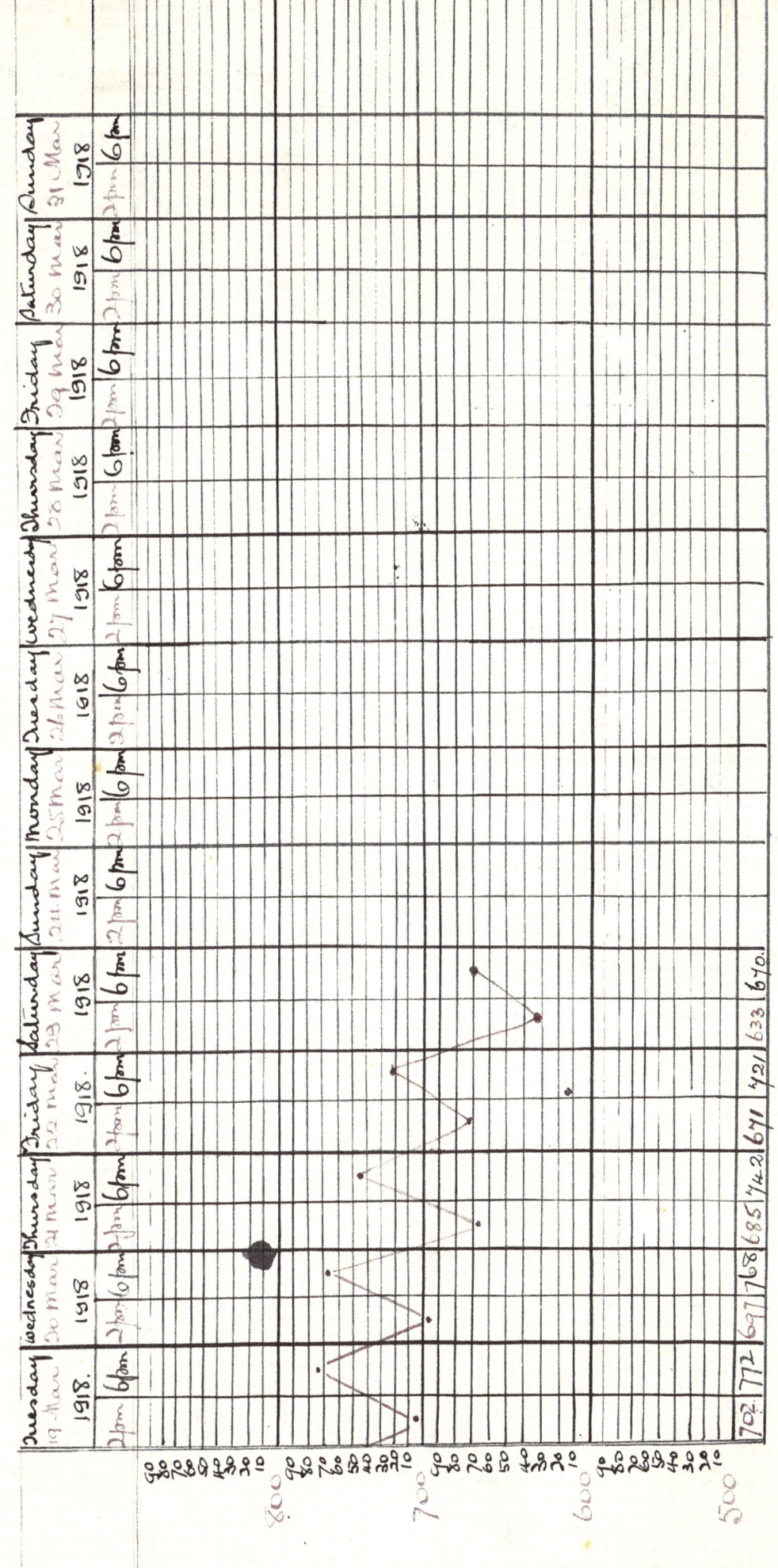

Chart showing No. of Cases of Scabies remaining in C.R.S. @ 2 p.m. & 6 p.m. daily.

Chart showing № of cases of Scabies remaining in CRS at 2pm & 6pm daily.

Friday 22 March 1918	Saturday 23 March 1918	Sunday 24 March 1918	Monday 25 March 1918	Tuesday 26 March 1918	Wednesday 27 March 1918	Thursday 28 March 1918	Friday 29 March 1918	Saturday 30 March 1918	Sunday 31 March 1918
2pm 6pm	2pm 6pm	2pm 6pm	2pm 6pm	2pm 6pm	2pm 6pm	2pm 6pm	2pm 6pm	2pm 6pm	6pm

140
130
120
110
100
90
80
70
60

58 46 62 62

WAR DIARY
or
INTELLIGENCE SUMMARY.

Confidential.

WAR DIARY
of
2/1st West Riding Field Ambce.
R.A.M.C. (T.)

Period April 1st to 30th inclusive. 1918

Volume XVI

140/2900

WAR DIARY or INTELLIGENCE SUMMARY

(Erase heading not required.)

Army Form C. 2118
2/1 R. Field Ambulance
R.A.M.C. (T.F.)

Place	Date	Hour	Summary of Events and Information	Remarks and references to Appendices
Sh.51c V17 b 7.2 LA CAUCHIE	1918 1st Mar.		Advance party sent to HENU	LAWR
	2nd "	4 p.m.	Unit moved to HENU – arrived 4 p.m. – Accommodation moderate	LAWR
Sheet 57d D19.a.6.9 HENU	3rd "		Sick of 186 Bde group collected & evacuated & arrangements made for this to be done daily	LAWR ADMS.4.M.M.1028/4/28
	4th "		Capt. N.N. Robinson R.G.M.C.(S.R.) struck off the strength of the Unit	LAWR
	5th "		Major H.G. Sweeten R.A.M.C.(S.R.) arrives & taken on strength of Unit	LAWR 62 2nd. RAM Coys. 37
	6th "		Instructions received for Unit to work to SOUASTRE on 8th inst.	LAWR ADMS. letter 7.iii.18
SOUASTRE Sh.57d D22.d.6.5	7th "		Main advance party sent to SOUASTRE to take over billets. Unit moved to SOUASTRE 24hrs. Advance party sent to each battalion of 186 Infy Bde. 2 Bearers Sub-divisions attached to 2/3 N.R. Fd. Ambce.	LAWR LAWR LAWR
	8th "		Sent to 2/3 N.R. Fd. Ambce A.D.S. BIENVILLERS. Three cars attached to 2/3 N.R. Fd. Ambce. Arrangements made for dealing with local sick & for their evacuation. Two N.C.Os & 28 men attached to 2/3 N.R. Fd. Ambce. at A.D.S. BIENVILLERS	LAWR LAWR
	10th "		Two officers & N.C.Os & 17 men held in readiness for duty at a C.C.S.	LAWR ADMS letter M1029/6
	11th "		Warning orders received to be prepared to open M.D.S. at PAS. in case of retirement to Purple Line. Suggested sites surveyed.	LAWR
	12th "		Lieut. J.G. JONES N.O.R.C., U.S.A. sent for duty to 310 Bde R.F.A. & struck off the strength of this Unit	LAWR ADMS M1029/10/5
	13th "		Investigated widely billets at PAS in event of moving there. Pte H. Langley killed in action & Pte J.R. Groves wounded	LAWR
	15 "		Pte J.R. Groves died of wounds	L.G.M.R.

Army Form C. 2118.

WAR DIARY
or
INTELLIGENCE SUMMARY.
(Erase heading not required.)

ORIGINAL.

Place	Date	Hour	Summary of Events and Information	Remarks and references to Appendices
Shed 57A D.22 A.6.5	1918		LAWR	
SOUASTRE	14th Apl		Lieut. A.P.N.SAGE M.O.R.C.U.S.A. 10 Officers, 2 N.C.Os & 12 men sent for temporary duty to No 3 CANADIAN STATIONARY HOSPITAL at DOULLENS	LAWR ADMS letter M7/46
			Capt. H.B. POPE & Capt. J.H. BLACKBURN M.C. promoted to rank of Acting Major as from 4th Jan. 1918	LAWR ADMS letter M73/5
	15th "		Major H.G. SMEETH returned to No 10 General Hospital & struck off strength of Unit.	LAWR ADMS letter M97
PAS Shed 57A C.22 a 7.8	17th "		Unit moved to PAS - Accommodation good.	LAWR
	18th "		Arrangements made for reception & evacuation of local sick - One reinforcement arrived	LAWR
	21 "		Attended Conference at A.D.M.S. Office - Lieut. F.J. COTLER R.A.M.C. (T.C.) reported for duty & taken on strength of Unit	LAWR A.D.M.S letter M 204
	22 "		Order received to move to MARIEUX on the 23rd	LAWR (2nd BN R.A.M.C. Ord. 39
	23 "		Inspected billets at MARIEUX - Pte J. NHILE wounded	LAWR
	24 "		Relief of bearers in forward area & return of same to Unit. Advance party sent to MARIEUX to take over billets from 50th Fd Amb.	LAWR
MARIEUX Shed 57A H.20 a.5.9	25th "		Advance party of 1 S.B. arrived to take over at PAS from 50 th Fd Amb. Unit moved to MARIEUX - Accommodation fairly good. Arrangements made for daily collection of sick at 185 Fd/1 Fd. Warning order received to prepare to send Bearer Division & 1 Fd Sub division to forward area at short notice.	LAWR A.D.M.S letter M2 1874/5.
	26th "		in case of Emergency	LAWR
			Officer i/c bearer division surveyed forward area of division. (Maj. N.B. POPE & Capt. N.D. PINKEN)	LAWR
	27th "		Site earmarked for C.R.S. MARIEUX - Visited D.D.M.S. in Corps re proposed site C.R.S.	LAWR
	29th "		Attended conference at A.D.M.S' Office	LAWR ADMS letter M32 sc

J. Walter Foster
LIEUT-COL R.A.M.C.(T)
2/1st W.R. FIELD AMBULANCE.

(MEDICAL)
Army Form C. 2118.

WAR DIARY
or
INTELLIGENCE SUMMARY.
(Erase heading not required.)

- Confidential -

WAR DIARY

of

2/1st West Riding Field Amb ce
R.A.M.C.(T)

Period 1st to 31st May inclusive

Volume XVII

ORIGINAL

140/2983

WAR DIARY or INTELLIGENCE SUMMARY.

(MEDICAL) Army Form C. 2118.

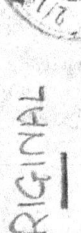

Place	Date	Hour	Summary of Events and Information	Remarks and references to Appendices
Sheet 57D MARIEUX H30 a.5.9.	1-5.V.18		Nothing to report.	L.L.WR
	6.V.18.		Horse transport inspected by A.D.M.S. & D.A.D.V.S.	L.L.WR
	7.V.18		Visited 2/1 M.A.C. at GEZAINCOURT - Inspected Car fitted up with Splints	L.G.W A.D.M.S. letter M386
	9.V.18		Attended Conference at Offices of A.D.M.S.	L.G.W
	13.V.18		Instructions received to work personnel to C.R.S. MARIEUX WOOD - hand to C.R.S. completed	L.G.W A.D.M.S. letter M/5/548
Sheet 57D MARIEUX WOOD	14.V.18		Orders received for Unit to work to SOUASTRE on 17th inst. & take over M.D.S. from 4 & 5 Field Ambulances 62nd Div R.A.M.C Order No. 41	L.L.WR
I.19.C.2.2			hand [?] completed by 5/- in our huddle - O.C. proceeded on 30 days Special leave to U.K.	L.L.WR
			Major H.B. POPE in command of Unit	
	15/5/18		Vided SOUASTRE anticipated M.D.S. arranged here at HENU. Arranged details [relief?].	off
	16/5/18		Advance Party - A/Major & 21 O.R. proceeded to SOUASTRE, Took over from 48th Field Ambulance	
			2 Bearer Squads to remain attached to each Infantry battalion of 185th Bde. (62nd Brig R.A.M.C operation orders No. 41)	off
SOUASTRE H25	17/5/18		Unit marched to SOUASTRE. One [?] established in the [Reserve?] Sub-division being taken over at HENU afterwards to through lines having 2 sub-divisions & preserving details in room at the M.D.S.	off
St Leg A D.22.a.7.2 Logie-hires Shed 57D D.13.d.4.4			Relief completed by 5 P.m.	

WAR DIARY
or
INTELLIGENCE SUMMARY.
(Erase heading not required.)

Army Form C. 2118.

ORIGINAL

Instructions regarding War Diaries and Intelligence Summaries are contained in F.S. Regs., Part II. and the Staff Manual respectively. Title pages will be prepared in manuscript.

Place	Date	Hour	Summary of Events and Information	Remarks and references to Appendices
	18/5/18		Continuous Aeroplane shelter commenced at Shrapnel hire as a protection against anti-aircraft shrapnel. The 8th Field Ambulance having had two horses wounded by this. Stand Post tracings to have been commenced.	D.H.A.
	19/5/18		Sandbagging of M.D.S. commenced, road drains & filling up horse shelter openings formed flew windows, etc.	
	20/5/18		Instructions issued regarding procedure in case of severe gas shell bombardment. A large allen made for post. D.M.S. III Army & D.D.M.S. 62 Div. inspected M.D.S. First relief of 2 bed subdivision at M.D.S. Empty subdivision in reserve at Shrapnel hire. Relief followed automatically after 3 hours periods for 2 hours each.	D.H.A.
	23/5/18		D.M.S. V. J. Ctd. M.D.S. Organised the deal with a large number of casualties, extra lotrines & shelters constructed.	Sketch 1/M/18 attached.
	24/5/18		Capt. H.D. Granter Lucferausin attached as M.O. 2/7 Br. Westryon Refs. (Appx. B/81s.)	D.H.A.
	27/5/18		Capt. R.P. Anderson took a Enemy Patients (Lance Corp 2/9 N.Staffshire Regt.) Ever Roads by M.D.S. shelled from 7.30 P.m. to 7.50 P.m. by 6" Hv. H.E. 5 Casualties including 3 Nurses.	D.H.A.
	28/5/18		3 Crash shearing fire on SOUASTRE at 5.0 A.m. 8.20 A.m. at 7 P.m.	D.H.A.
	29/5/18		Dugout shelling following up	D.H.A.

Army Form C. 2118.

WAR DIARY
or
INTELLIGENCE SUMMARY.
(Erase heading not required.)

ORIGINAL

Instructions regarding War Diaries and Intelligence Summaries are contained in F. S. Regs., Part II. and the Staff Manual respectively. Title pages will be prepared in manuscript.

Place	Date	Hour	Summary of Events and Information	Remarks and references to Appendices
SOUASTRE	30/9/15		Aujm Rubin Irving [signature] — Major Rennie 2/1st W.R. Field Ambulance.	S.F.

- M.D.S. - SOUASTRE -

Plan of System of Admission
and Evacuation of Patients -

MEDICAL

WAR DIARY
or
INTELLIGENCE SUMMARY.
(Erase heading not required.)

Army Form C. 2118.

— CONFIDENTIAL —

WAR DIARY

of

2/1st West Riding Field Ambce.

Period :- 1st to 30th June
1918.

Volume
XVIII

ORIGINAL

46/30/6.

MEDICAL
ORIGINAL

WAR DIARY
or
INTELLIGENCE SUMMARY.
(Erase heading not required.)

Army Form C. 2118.

Instructions regarding War Diaries and Intelligence Summaries are contained in F. S. Regs., Part II. and the Staff Manual respectively. Title pages will be prepared in manuscript.

Place	Date	Hour	Summary of Events and Information	Remarks and references to Appendices
S7 D. D.22.a.7.2 A.DS. SOUASTRE	1/6/18		ADMS visited A.D.S. 3 Officers attended lecture on Trench fever given by Corps Chemical Adviser at 62nd Div Hdqrs. A.T.S. &W. received admin station conveniences, NCOTIS's to bring given in their area.	ibid
	2/6/18		Harassing shell fire in vicinity A.DS.	ibid
	3/6/18		Work commenced on new A.DS on SOUASTRE - ST AMAND Road. (5 bomb shelters shelters let into ibid side of Ditch bank in convenient situation for roads & improved com country track) accommodation when completed for about 40 stretcher cases. 3 Army instructions regarding situation Medical Units. QC/10370 of 1/6/18 (62nd Bn M/1039/40 of 3/6/16) received relating being noted when	ibid
Coy S7 D. D.22.a.4.6	4/6/18		A.DS moved to temporary premises pending completion of new work. Sketch plan improved attached.	ibid
	5/6/18		Temporary premises inspected by ADM.S	ibid
	9/6/18		Majors Giles, & Lieuts Edwards, R.O. R.C. U.S.A. reported for duty. Posted to the 3/4 the R.P.	ibid
	10/6/18		Promotions received for Lieut. F.J. Carter R.A.M.C. T.C. to report to O.C 2/4 the Hant's Reg, as no is returning from special leave.	ibid
	14/6/18		Capt H.A. Mackenzie M.C. reported horse 2/4 Cov Hant's for temporary duty.	ibid
	15/1/18		Capt R. P Anderson M.C. reported horse 26 A Field Amb. R.A.M for temporary duty.	ibid
	6/6/18		Gun accessor selection received for trial, in the casualties (above shaneuvring by stretcher in Bdens.	ibid

WAR DIARY
or
INTELLIGENCE SUMMARY.
(Erase heading not required.)

Army Form C. 2118.

Place	Date	Hour	Summary of Events and Information	Remarks and references to Appendices
Hunts? P	19/6/18		Lieut. F.J. Curtis R.A.M.C. T.C. returned from special leave	AA C
D.22.a.4.6	20/6/18		and relieved Captain A. Mackenzie in No. 1. 2/6 Bn. Hants Reg. relieving 1/1 Shropshire Light	AA C
SOUASTRE	22/6/18		A.D.S. opened work inspected by D.D.M.S. 4th Corps.	AA C
			62nd Bri. R.A.M.C. Operation Order No. 43. received instructing this Unit to move A.D.S. to 49th	
			Field Ambulance on 25/6/18. Also moved on relief to Rest Station at THIEVRES.	AA C
	24/6/18		Unit at THIEVRES inspected Lecture Class. Practised stretcher	AA C
THIEVRES	25/6/18		A.D.S. handed over. Relief completed by 12 noon. Unit arrived at THIEVRES. Took over	AA C
Sect 57 P			Main Rest House at PAS from OC 2/3 West Riding Field Ambulance.	
T.1.A.2.4	26/6/18		G.O.C. division inspected billets. While in Corps reserve the 2/1st West Riding Field Ambulance	AA C
			would be responsible for evacuation of wounded from the Rest Line, being affiliated to 186th Field	
			Ambulance. Provisional Scheme Reference received.	
	27/6/18		Captain D. Forbes M.C. & 1 Lieut. A'Lea proceeded to in patient Rest Line to forward area	AA C
			suspected A.D.S. Site ordered ADS. Captain A. Mackenzie R.A.C. proceeded on ordinary leave to	
			U.K. 62 ? rifle team received regarding the present installed in G.H.Q. reserve.	
	28/6/18		Major Mc Rae MD., Major Learmonth M.C. R.A.M.C. inspected Rest Line forward area C	AA C
			forward provisional Site for ADS ordinary standing SOS.	

[signature] Major Wright
OC 2/1st W.R. FIELD AMBULANCE

Army Form C. 2118.

WAR DIARY
or
INTELLIGENCE SUMMARY.
(Erase heading not required.)

Instructions regarding War Diaries and Intelligence Summaries are contained in F. S. Regs., Part II. and the Staff Manual respectively. Title pages will be prepared in manuscript.

Place	Date	Hour	Summary of Events and Information	Remarks and references to Appendices
Rst 5 D. T.1.d.2.4.				
THIEVRES	29/4/16		Work at A.D.S. SOUASTRE from receiving station. Had a horse case. Immediate effect good. Saline infusion begun on leaving R.A.P. A total of 160 slightly gassed cases only received during the two hours at the A.D.S. ("cheers"), mainly bruises.	

f.o.t. [signature] Major [illegible]

f.o.t. 2/1ST W.R. FIELD AMBULANCE.

Temporary Res. D.22.a.4.6.
Sheet 57D.

[Stamp: 2/1 W.R. FIELD AMBULANCE R.A.M.C. (T.F.)]

To St Amand →

To Souastre →

Cellar

Stretcher Cases

Park for Motor Ambulances

Sick Room

Park for Motor Ambulances

Orderly Room

Q.M. Stores | Evacuation Room

Water Cart Stand

Dispensary

Cook-house

Gassed Cases

DISPOSITION OF M.D.S.
— SOUASTRE —

MEDICAL

Army Form C. 2118.

WAR DIARY
or
INTELLIGENCE SUMMARY.
(Erase heading not required.)

Instructions regarding War Diaries and Intelligence Summaries are contained in F.S. Regs., Part II. and the Staff Manual respectively. Title pages will be prepared in manuscript.

Place	Date	Hour	Summary of Events and Information	Remarks and references to Appendices

CONFIDENTIAL

July 1918

WAR DIARY

of

2/1st WEST RIDING FIELD AMBCE.
R.A.M.C. (T).

Period 1st – 31st July 1918.

Volume XIX

140/3/31.

COMMITTEE FOR THE
MEDICAL HISTORY OF THE WAR
Date 6 SEP. 1918

WAR DIARY
or
INTELLIGENCE SUMMARY
(Erase heading not required.)

Army Form C. 2118.

ORIGINAL

Place	Date	Hour	Summary of Events and Information	Remarks and references to Appendices
THIEVRES	1/7/18		Advance Party sent from THIEVRES to take over the M.D.S. AUTHIE which was being vacated	App
SD.I.I.d.0.4			as a Corps Rest Station (62nd Div. RAMC Order No 44), handed by 3rd New Zealand Field Amb.	
CRS AUTHIE	2/7/18		Unit less Advance Party moved to CRS AUTHIE. M.D.S. Took over the books etc	App
SD.I.S:6.2.9			C.R.S. at 12 noon. Accommodation for, say, for about 250 patients.	
	4/7/18		The appointment of an Officer in each Division to test shocked cases at A.D.S.s by firing below	App
			in/was considered. Capt L.A. Mackenzie recommended for this. Usual training employment.	
	8/7/18		Qr Mr Capt Lawton proceed to U.K. on ordinary leave.	App
			Temporary medical charge of 1/704 + 9th Labour groups during absence 1/Mo's concerned.	
	10/7/18		1st Lieut A.R.E. Edwards proceeded as Mo i/c 9th Bn. Tank Corps relieving M Sharpe.	App
			Capt. R.P. Anderson R.A.M.C.(T) M.C. noted as Mo i/c 312th Bde R.F.A. whom Mckay R	App
	13/7/18		Warning Order received to be prepared to move by Statistical train 14/7/18 Starting 2 Pm	App
	14/7/18		62nd Bn. Wires left three CA.S. handed over to Field Ambulance of 37 Bn.	
			C.R.S. handed over to 2nd New Zealand Field Ambulance at 12 noon.	
			Order to move to XXII British Corps area received (RAMC Orders No 45) under detailed	
			instructions of 187th Inf Bde. Unit with Statistical Field Ambulance was affiliated with Time	
	15/7/18		These detailed instructions received evening of 14/7/18, Unit arrived M 3.20 Pm Detrained	App

Army Form C. 2118.

ORIGINAL

WAR DIARY
or
INTELLIGENCE SUMMARY.
(Erase heading not required.)

Instructions regarding War Diaries and Intelligence Summaries are contained in F. S. Regs., Part II. and the Staff Manual respectively. Title pages will be prepared in manuscript.

Place	Date	Hour	Summary of Events and Information	Remarks and references to Appendices
In Train	15/7/16		DOULLENS NORTH. Train moved out 9.30 A.m. Route followed AMIENS → BEAUVAIS → PERSAN → PARIS → LAROCHE → ST. FLORENTIN → TROYES → ARCIS → SOMMESOUS train	Ry. Master Doullens
	16/7/16		Unit detrained. Marched to SOUDRON arriving 10.55 P.m. Billeted in the village. Journey uneventful.	DHJ
SOUDRON	17/7/16		March resumed to BISSEUIL arriving 11.45 P.m. Latter part of march in dusk thunderstorm	DHJ
BISSEUIL	18/7/16		2 Bearer Squads & 1 nurse attached to each Battalion 1/187 & 2/A. Ade. 1 Officer & and Subdivision left for forward area. 1 Officer & Hardy left for A.D.S. SERMIERS, in DAIMLER Ambulance	DHJ
	19/7/16		Remainder of Unit moved to ST. IMOGES arriving 3 P.m. Bivouaced in wood near village. One last Subdivision sent to A.D.S. SERMIERS – killed No. 28 in main Street by church. MAJOR POPE visited A.D.S. TELEGRAMS sent to Bearer Officers giving details of visits of A.D.S. Suggested booking both as front A.D.S.	
ST IMOGES	20/7/16		MDS opened at North end of village & St IMOGES. Routine observed on Sketch.	Sketch of MDS Arrangements
	21/7/16		1 Tent Subdivision & 2/2 West Riding Field Ambulance attached to M.O.S. (or day).	
	22/7/16		807 Cases during 24 hours. Officers Opening Attack, Camp shelled.	
	23/7/16		401 Cases during Succeeding 24 hours (approx) Camp shelled 3.02 a.m. now 22" howitzer 23rd.	

Army Form C. 2118.

WAR DIARY
or
INTELLIGENCE SUMMARY.

(Erase heading not required.)

ORIGINAL

Instructions regarding War Diaries and Intelligence Summaries are contained in F. S. Regs., Part II. and the Staff Manual respectively. Title pages will be prepared in manuscript.

Place	Date	Hour	Summary of Events and Information	Remarks and references to Appendices
ST. IMOGES	24/7/18		Number of Bearers from 2/3rd between 24 & 341. Village bombed.	Apx.
	25/7/18		1 Bearer subdivision still subdivision relieved in forward area	Apx.
	26/7/18		Capt. A. Mackenzie M.C. attached subdivision proceeded to forward area.	Apx.
	27/7/18		Lieut. Col. W. Lilie proceeded to England (62 Div. Letter A/10/25-/27).	Apx.
	28/7/18		Lieut. R.G. Giles proceeded to duty as No. 1/c a/Ton D.H.I. (R. Rean)	Apx.
			(A/pend. letter M 802. 28/7/18).	
	29/7/18		D.C.M.S. inspected A.D.S.	
	30/7/18		62 Div. R.A.M.C. Training Order No. 1 obtaining received. Capt. A. Mackenzie bearer subdivision returned from forward area. 1st Lieut. R.G. Giles a/Ton M.O. 9th Ryle fluid. Bearer Squad attached to stabilers of 187 "Inf. Bde returned.	Apx.
	31/7/18		Throughout the whole action Rennes attacks Amiens rendered every possible assistance to the wounded. Services late at A.D.S. after SERMIERS.	Apx.

F. Mille
MAJOR. R.A.M.C.(T)
2/1st W.R. FIELD AMBULANCE.

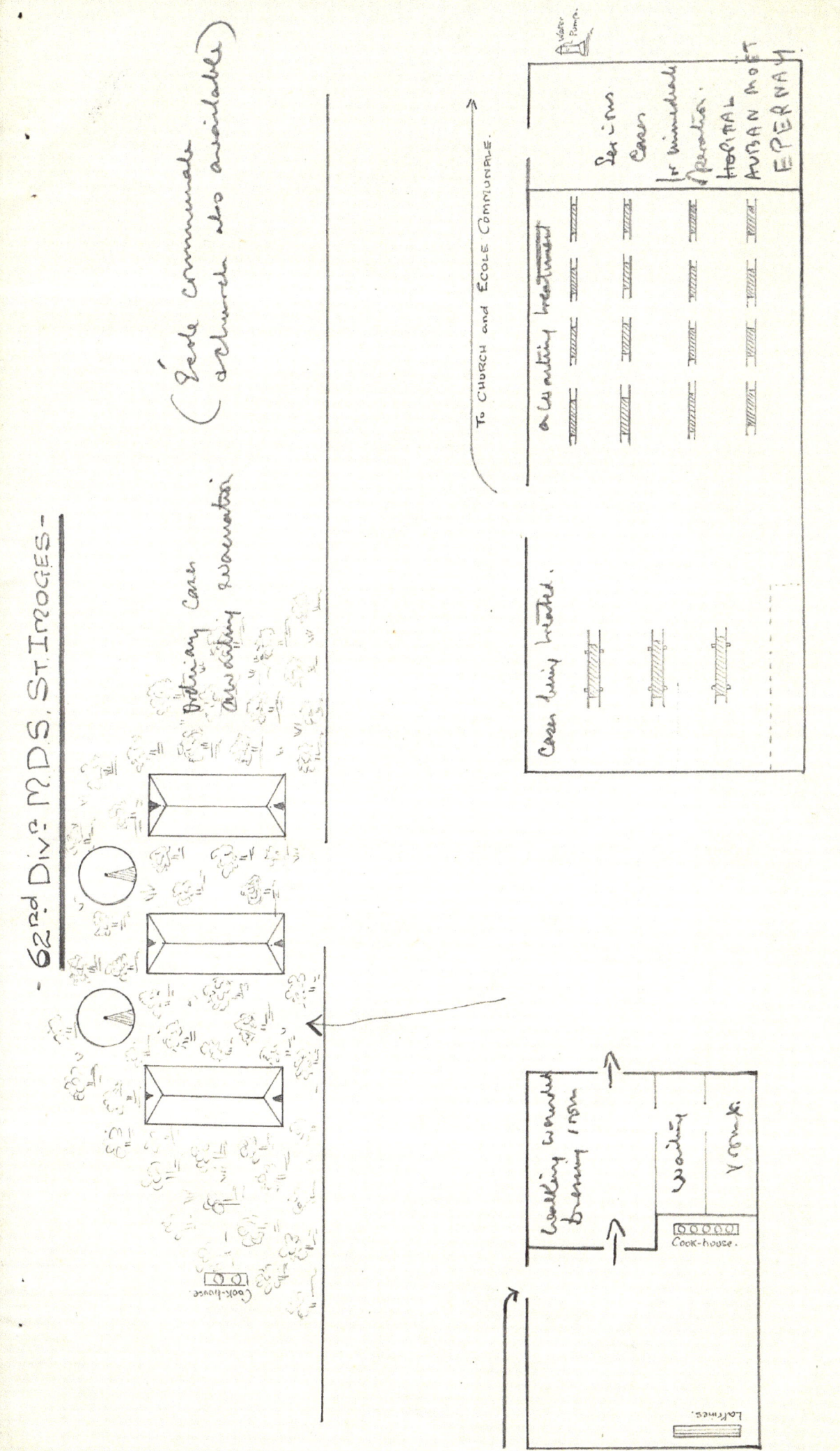

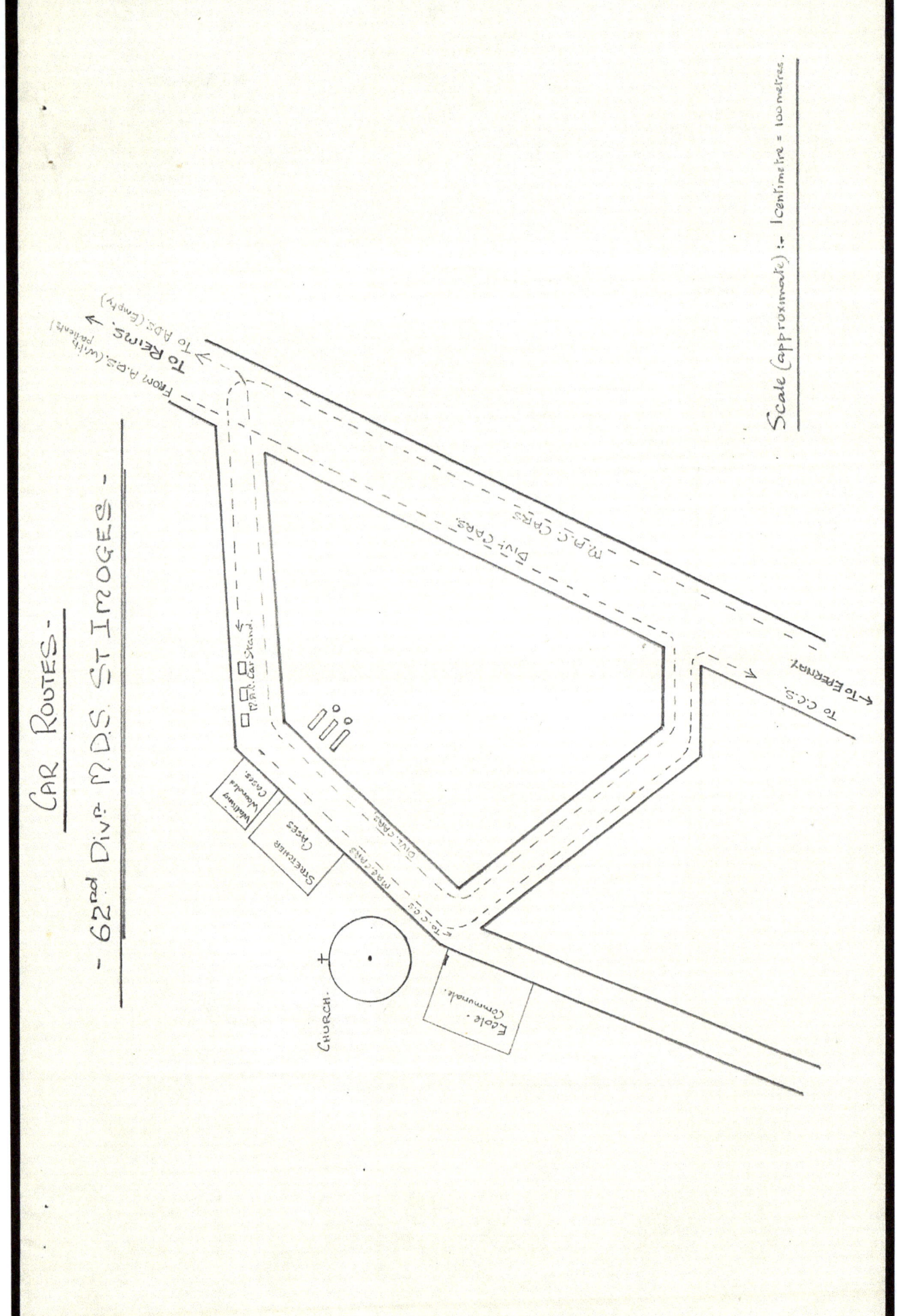

SECRET   Copy No_____

OPERATION ORDERS BY LIEUT. COL. SALTER LISTER,
COMMANDING 2/1ST WEST RIDING FIELD AMBCE.

Ref. Map Sheet LENS 11

14th July, 1918.

The 187th Infantry Brigade to which this Unit is at present attached will move on the 14th and 15th inst by strategical trains. Entrainment will be carried out in accordance with the following instructions.

Entraining Station:— DOULLENS NORTH

(a) Refers to Officers' Mess House, P/S, and has been issued to Capt. H. S. Pickles, M.C.

(b) A Horse Ambulance to report at Brigade Headquarters, GOUIN, at 8 a.m. with Driver, one Orderly. Dress:— Full Marching Order. One day's ration for man and two horses to be carried. They will receive their orders at Brigade Headquarters and remain at DOULLENS NORTH until the Field Ambulance arrives.

Second Horse Ambulance to report at 2.30 p.m. at GOUIN to O.C. 2/4th Batt. K.O.Y.L.I. and remain at DOULLENS NORTH as above.

Third Horse Ambulance to report at 6.30 p.m. at GOUIN to O.C. 2/4th Batt. York & Lancs. and remain at DOULLENS NORTH as above.

(c) A Ford Car to report to R.T.O. at DOULLENS NORTH at 10.30 a.m. to remove any casualties during entrainment to C.C.S. Dress:— Full Marching Order. One day's ration to be carried. The Car will remain there until receiving further instructions.

(d) Horse Ambulances are not available for the transport of Baggage. A large amount of Baggage normally carried will therefore be dumped at DOULLENS NORTH, being taken by Motor Lorry. One N.C.O. will accompany lorry and will be shown where to dump stores by R.T.O. *He will carry the unexpended portion of the days ration & two additional days rations.*

(e) An Entraining Officer will report to Brigade representative at DOULLENS NORTH (probably Lieut. Beetham, M.C. 2/4 York & Lancs) 3½ hours before departure of train and ½ hour before transport arrives, i.e. Entraining Officer reports 4 a.m., Transport arrives 4.30 a.m., Train departs 7.40 a.m. *Main Body arrives 6 a.m.*

Entraining Officer will have an Entraining State (in duplicate) as follows:—

No. of Officers
No. of O. Ranks
N. of animals
No. of 2 Wheeled Vehicles
No. of 4 "   "   "   (to include Supply & Baggage
                                                 Wagons.)
No. of Ambulance Cars

Loading Party and Unloading Party detailed by Battalions.
Transport will not enter station until consent of Brigade Entraining Officer is given.

The Train is serial No. 10 (Train No. 182) and contains Field Ambulance, Sang Divnl. Employment Coy. and Cable Section.

Horses will be watered before entrainment.
The unit will provide ropes for tying up horses in the trucks.
Horses will be unharnessed, harness stacked in the middle of each truck and two men must travel in each truck.

The unexpended portion of day's ration will be on the man. Supplies for the following day will be carried on train, i.e. the Unit will have rations for Sunday, Monday and ~~Tuesday~~ *Thursday*
Water Carts to be full.
A train ration will be issued at Entraining Station and loaded on to train by our own unit.

OPERATION ORDERS (Contd. No. 2)

3.20.
3.20.

(f) **Main Body.** To be at DOULLENS NORTH at 6 a.m.
Dress:- Full Marching Order. Soft caps will be worn,
Steel Helmets carried on right shoulder, water bottles full,
unexpended portion of the day's ration and iron rations will
be carried on the man.

On arrival, O.C. will inform and Unit will not enter
platform until permission has been obtained from Brigade
Entraining Officer.

Horses to be watered before entrainment and ropes for
tying up in trucks carried. Horses to be unsaddled as
before.

Supplies for Monday and ~~Tuesday~~ Thursday on wagons.

On arrival at destination troops to be marched clear
of station as soon as possible. Major J T Blackburn, M.C.,
Unit Billeting Officer, will probably be waiting at destination.

Time taken to get to DOULLENS - 2½ hours.

A train ration will be issued at the Entraining Station
and will be loaded by our own unit.

(Signed) WALTER LISTER
Lieut. Col. RAMC(T)
2/1st West Riding Field Ambulance.

Copies to:-
1. O.C.
2. Major H. R. Pope
3. Capt. L. A. Mackenzie, M.C.
4. Capt. H. S. Pickles, M.C.
5. 1st/Lieut. R. C. Giles, MORC USA
6. Q.M.S. Kendall
7. S/M. Kelly
8. C.M.S. Wordsworth
9. Sergt. Clark
10. Office

After Order

(g) **Motor Transport** 1 Daimler and 2 Fords will
report to R.T.O. DOULLENS at 1.30 p.m. to-day and be
loaded on trains on which there are empty flats.
Cpl. Ashley will be in charge of the detachment.
Personnel will be in Full Marching Order with the
unexpired portion of to-day's ration and other two
days' rations.

Train moves
9.42 pm ~~to-morrow~~ 16/7/18
~~to-morrow~~ 16/7/18

3 Daimlers will report to R.T.O. SAULTY at 5.12 p.m.
Rations etc. as before (For 2nd M.T. Train No. 35).
3 Daimlers will report to R.T.O. SAULTY at 10.12 p.m.
to go by 3rd M.T. Train No. 36, moving out at 2.42 am
16/7/18. The M.T. Sergt. will distribute Stores equally
between the Ambulances. (Rations as before).

(h) **Amendment to para. (e) concerning rations**
The train ration therein referred to are the
rations for the 16th and 17th i.e. ~~Tuesday~~ TUESDAY & ~~Friday~~ WEDNESDAY and
will be dumped at the station by Divisional Train. 1 Officer
to be detailed later with Sergt. Hirst & Fatigue Party of this
Unit will load them on to one of the trucks. The Officer
i/c will report that this has been done to the O.C. and the
Entraining Officer.

Walter Lister
LIEUT-COL

MEDICAL

Army Form C. 2118.

WAR DIARY
or
INTELLIGENCE SUMMARY.
(Erase heading not required.)

Instructions regarding War Diaries and Intelligence Summaries are contained in F. S. Regs., Part II. and the Staff Manual respectively. Title pages will be prepared in manuscript.

Vol 20
Med/3200.

— Confidential —

WAR DIARY
— of —
2/1st
2/1 West Riding Field Ambulance

Period 1st to 31st Aug/1918.

Volume XIX

Aug 1918

Place	Date	Hour	Summary of Events and Information	Remarks and references to Appendices

WAR DIARY
or
INTELLIGENCE SUMMARY.
(Erase heading not required.)

Army Form C. 2118.

Instructions regarding War Diaries and Intelligence Summaries are contained in F.S. Regs., Part II. and the Staff Manual respectively. Title pages will be prepared in manuscript.

Original

Place	Date	Hour	Summary of Events and Information	Remarks and references to Appendices
Arrt Rct CHALONS 1050 St. IROGES	Aug 1st		Unit left H.T. St. IROGES marched via AVENAY to BISSEVIL arriving there. H.T. Col-	Atd
	2nd		Other over Party to advance Party. 187th Inf. Bde. order to entrain at AVIZE, from No. 24 at 6.26 P.M. 4/8/18, & to Bivouac HENU-COUIN area on arrival in IV British Corps Area.	Atd
	3rd		Advertising Party detailed, travelled by train No. 2 departing 8.26 P.M.	Atd
	4th		Loading Party proceeded for BISSEVIL to AVIZE reporting 3.6 P.M. Main body here leaving Ladorenne Parker reported at AVIZE 5.6 P.M., train ordered up 6.26 P.M. Unit transported proceeded independently to SOMMESOUS Station entrained. Rations carried to midnight 6/8/18.	Atd
	5–6		Train proceeded via SEZANNE – NOGENT – PANTIN – BEAUVAIS – AMIENS – BOULLENS – CONDICOURT arriving there 1 P.M. 6/8/18. Detrained marched to VAUCHELLES–LES–AUTIE, billets there	Atd
VAUCHELLES	7th		2 officers M.R.C., USA reported for duty (RD.W.S. No. 923/1) Lieut C.T. SCURRY & Lieut A.H. GWYNN	Atd
Ant S.5.D T:32.6.9.8	8th		Sick collected in Brigade area returned overnight.	Atd
	9th		10 reinforcements received 185th Infantry Brigade Provisional defence scheme received, the Division being in IV Corps left reserve in G.H.Q. Reserve.	Atd
	11th		Actual arrangements for provisional defence scheme received	Atd
	12th		1 officer proceeded to U.K. on ordinary leave. 2 officers & several N.C.O's surveyed rest line, (etc)	Atd

T2134. Wt. W708–776. 500000. 4/15. Sir J. C. & S.

Army Form C. 2118.

WAR DIARY
or
INTELLIGENCE SUMMARY.
(Erase heading not required.)

Instructions regarding War Diaries and Intelligence Summaries are contained in F.S. Regs., Part II. and the Staff Manual respectively. Title pages will be prepared in manuscript.

Original

Place	Date	Hour	Summary of Events and Information	Remarks and references to Appendices
VACELLES T.32.c.9.8	August 12th		(the latin alluded to defence scheme to 183 Inf Bde.)	App.
	13th		10 am A.R.E. U.S.A.— Lieut R.J.M. Louis reported for duty (Appd M.123)	App.
			3 Micro theatre mev's surveyed but defence line.	
	14th		Instructions received to instr. manning front line on 13th (Ph.III/3) cancelled. Same day by	App.
			M.39/A.	
	15th		2/s-Ln. Montgomery having been discharged from Ordnance Mess (Capt. J.M. Pringle) reported	App.
			for duty; and received equipment later but sent in to Advance dept. Ordnance Stores.	
			Addendum to Divisional defence scheme received.	
	16th	4 p.m.	62nd Bde. (temp.) warning order No. G.9 regarding order for SPURY received. 183 Inf. Bde.	App.
			order No. 124 received regarding order. Billeting party proceeded to determine them.	
			Destined — LOUVENCOURT — Main Body less advance party arrived 8.45 p.m., accommodated	
			under canvas at west entrance to village.	
LOUVENCOURT T.34.D.6.1.1	19th		183 Inf Bde. Orders No. 8 to move to VI Corps area. Billeting party proceeded BOURNERA	App.
			Unit less advance party arrived 2.10 p.m. 20/8/16. Route AUTIE, P.O.S., BONDCOURT.	
			Capt. Pringle proceeded on 10 months leave to UK.	
BOURNERA T.37.a.8.1 Q.6.c.8.1	20th		183 Inf. Bde. orders No. 7 regarding move to LA CAVETIE. Unit less advance party arrived at	App.

WAR DIARY
or
INTELLIGENCE SUMMARY

Army Form C. 2118.

Original

Place	Date	Hour	Summary of Events and Information	Remarks and references to Appendices
Rest S.C. Tip 2.9.1.	August 20th			
	21st	1.20 Am	LA COUCATE. Route POMMERA - LATHEUERE - LACOUCATE.	
			1 Officer proceeded on temporary duty to No. 40 C.C.S. PREVENT (Adm. 42/A)	Ad
			183rd Inf. Bde RAMC BMS + 132 received to base hire to IV Corps area, Billetry Parls	
SD 22nd			Proceeded to VAUCELLES. Unit in advance party arrived 2 A.m.	
			Two reinforcements arrived. Officer returned from 48 C.C.S. PREVENT.	Ado
Ref FN C.49 23rd			183 Inf. Bde order No 8 regarding move to St AMAND B.C. 4 Unit arrived 12 midnight 23/24	Add
ST AMAND AYETTE	24th		Unit proceeded at 8.27 a.m with 183 Inf. Bde to AYETTE through hira chern.	
			Personnel dismounted. Horse dale No 52 received 1. W.M. to detail 2 grooms remain	
			as usual to Sec Ambulancia. 9/183 Inf. Bde. 48/B2.1. 10 Men proceeded to Adv Bdy to	
			act in haison Officers. This unit also responsible for clearing the forward area. See	
			Unit proceeded to reconnoitre forward area.	
COURCELLES	25th		All remaining officer's 1 MO. 1 Attache, 1 Bearer Officer in Proceeded to form new Adv. Stn at	Ad
A6.d.8.5. Inf Rest S.C.NW			COURCELLES A.16.d.8.5. in quarry under canvas. 187 186 Inf Bde. in line, 183rd Inf Bde.	
			reserve. R.A.P's thus rigoneutin of 186 Bde on right specially accomadatus, this being done	
			doubt as to the station Wen-RAP's & blue mind which were always in action. Remainty	
			of 183 Bde in life line for Bayer Breakdown. See allowed upon 05.1.	Report No 1

Army Form C. 2118.

Original

WAR DIARY
or
INTELLIGENCE SUMMARY.
(Erase heading not required.)

Instructions regarding War Diaries and Intelligence Summaries are contained in F. S. Regs., Part II. and the Staff Manual respectively. Title pages will be prepared in manuscript.

Place	Date	Hour	Summary of Events and Information	Remarks and references to Appendices
CURCELLES A.D.S. A.16.d.8.5. Ind Pdsn S.7d N.W.	August 26		See attached report No 2 & No 3 Asy	Att Report No 2
				Att Report No 3
				Att Report No 4
	27"		See attached report No. 5	Att Report No 5
	28"		See attached report No. 6	Att Report No 6
	29"		See attached report No. 9	Att Report No 9
	30		See attached report No. 7	Att Report No 7
	31		See attached report No. 8	Att Report No 8

[signature] Major Commanding

2/1ST W.R. FIELD AMBULANCE

[Stamp: 2/1 W.R. FIELD AMBULANCE R.A.M.C. (T.F.)]

Copy.

Report No 1.

A.D.M.S.
62nd Division.

187th Infantry Brigade is clearing along ERVILLERS-COURCELLES Road., road good and Daimler Cars running forward over half the way to ERVILLERS. Bearers and Stretcher Wheels working between Loading Post and R.A.Ps.

Left R.A.Ps. in line. { 2/4 Y&Lancs.   B. 8. c. 2.2.
187th Inf. Bde.   { 5th Koyli.s.   B. 13. c. 2.1.
                   { 4th KOYLI.   moving up from Embankment

Right R.A.Ps. in line.   5th Dukes.   A. 29. c. 7. (?) G. 6. c. 7. 9.
186th Inf. Bde.   moving off to (?) G. 6. c. 7. 9.

2/4 Hants.   In cutting just below level X at A. 28. a. 9. 1.

2/4 Dukes.   Just above level X.

A car of the 3rd Division was stationed at this level crossing & the few cases which these M.Os had were sent this way. A Daimler has been sent here, & the place visited. Bearer squads in GOMIECOURT in cellars at A. 29. A. 3.8, very few cases

185th Infantry Brigade in Reserve.

It was understood from D.A.D.M.S. 62nd Division that walking wounded would be collected in lorries at the old A.D.S. at A. 15. a. 3.2. We are sending them there by Horse Ambce.

The A.D.S. is clear, & so are R.A.Ps.

(Signed) H.B.Pope.
Major. R.A.M.C.

25. -8- 18.

Report No. 2.

A.D.M.S. 62nd Division.

The following are the routes of evacuation of the right & left sectors respectively.

5th Duke of Wellington's R.A.P. G. 6. c. 7.9. by wheeled stretcher or hand carriage to relay in GOMIECOURT. A. 29. & 2.7. thence to car Loading Post at A. 22. c. 8. 4 to A.D.S.

2/4 Duke of Wellington's R.A.P. in Railway Embankment at A 28. a. 9.3, to car loading post on level crossing adjacent, thence to A.D.S. This R.A.P. is likely to move forward shortly to region of previous one.

2/4 Hants R.A.P. in railway cutting at A 25. b. 9. 11. evacuation as above.

These cars have been ordered to come to this A.D.S. although a little roundabout, instead of going direct to Dressing Station of old A.D.S. at A. 20. b. 5. d. (unless for good cause.)

Left Sector.

2/4 Koyli, R.A.P. Chalk Pit on ERVILLERS - MORY Road, then by hand carriage to Ford Car Loading Post at B. 13. c. 7. 5, thence to Daimler Loading Post at A. 18. c. 5. 6. The M.O. has 4 Bearer Squads.

5th KOYLI. R.A.P. B. 13. c. 1. 1. carry to Daimler Car Loading Post. This R.A.P. will move forward shortly.

2/4 Y&Lancs., R.A.P. B. 8. c. 2.2. by Ford (fetched by runner), or stretcher wheels, thence to Daimler Loading Post.

R.A.Ps. & A.D.S. remain clear.

(Signed) H.B.Pope.
Major. R.A.M.C.

26. 8. 18.
9. 30. am.

Report No 3.

A.D.M.S. 62nd Division.

The R.A.P's of the 186th Inf. Bde have been visited by me this morning & have moved as follows:-

R.A.P. 2/4 Hants in sunken road at A.30.c.9.1. The M.O is looking for another Aid Post in the neighbourhood of WATERLOT FARM, H.1.d.5.2.

R.A.P. 5th Duke of Wellington's in bluff at G.6.c.8.0.

R.A.P. 2/4 Duke of Wellington's. Still in railway cut Level X – A.28.a.9.2. but out of action. The M.O is looking for an R.A.P. further forward. Aid Posts clear. Daimlers run to light railway X at G.6.b.11.0. within a few yards therefore of the two active R.A.P's.

The ERVILLERS sector has not yet been visited this morning.

2.25 p.m.
26.8.18.

Report No 4

A.D.M.S. 62nd Division.

The following is the situation of R.A.P's of left sector (187 Inf Bde)

2/4 Y & Lancs. }
2/4 K.O.Y.L.I. } unchanged.

5th K.O.Y.L.I. B.27.a.9.4, in sunken road.

The two former evacuate to Ford Loading Post at B.13.b.8.6, thence to Daimler Loading Post at A.18.c.4.7 thence to A.D.S. This COURCELLES – ERVILLERS road has become so bad that it is proposed to move the A.D.S. to the Chateau GOMIECOURT tomorrow. There are two rooms – a large dug-out & a cellar under the house. The ERVILLERS – GOMIECOURT Road is in excellent condition & this change will enable Daimlers to run to the present Ford Loading Post, besides allowing A.D.S. work to be carried on under better conditions.

Right Sector R.A.P's.
5th Duke of Wellington's in bluff at G.6.b.8.0.
2/4th Duke of Wellington's in same bluff a few yards away.
A Daimler Car stands at the door of each R.A.P. travelling along the GOMIECOURT – SAPIGNIES Road to the light railway in A.30.d, thence by fair-weather track to R.A.P. These cars also receive the cases from 5th K.O.Y.L.I., three squads carrying from the R.A.P. at B.27.a.9.4 to a relay at the light railway X at B.26.a.1.8. (the old watering point is here, & the tank on the wooden framework is a good landmark) from the Railway Crossing to the cars at the Duke of Wellington's R.A.P's in the bluff.

The roads leading to BEHAGNIES & SAPIGNIES have been inspected this afternoon, also, & the intervening main BAPAUME – ERVILLERS road, they are fairly good, & it is proposed tomorrow to run cars if necessary into the main road through SAPIGNIES. Since returning from this round, news has been received that the M.O. of the 2/4 Hants has moved to H.3.b.2.7.

(signed) H.B. Pope.
Major R.A.M.C.

10.30 pm.
26.-8.-18.

Copy

Report No 5.

Map Sheet No 57.C.N.W.

A.D.M.S. 62nd Division.

Evacuation of 187th Inf Bde. R.A.Ps.

(1). 2/4 Y.Lancs. B.8. c. 2.2 as before. Daimler Loading Post B.13. c. 8.6, + direct to A.D.S. or calling on Capt Mackenzie at B.13. d. 1.5 where a Ford Car also waits for local casualties.

(2). 2/4 KoyLI in sunken road B.15. d. 0.5 by railway, thence to ~~railway~~ relay at old R.A.P. about B.14. d. 4.4. in Chalk Pit (the previous R.A.P. of this Unit.) + Daimler loading Post.

(3). 5 KoyLI in bluff about B.28. a. 5.8. thence to relay in old O.P. about B.27. a. 2.1, thence to Ford Loading Post at Water Point B.26. a. 1. 8. thence via ERVILLERS. Major Wrigglesworth is staying at this Water Point tonight where a bricked tunnel exists under the road.

Evacuation of 186th Bde. R.A.Ps.

5 Duke of Wellingtons. Sunken road at H.2. c. 6.4.
2/4 Hants, in bluff at H.H. a. 4. 8. (5 squads attached as carry is long + no relay post exists.)
Daimler Loading Post by Church in BEHAGNIES - H.1.C.o.2.
Cases can be stored in Cinema Theatre (Brick arched roof) + a deep dug out close by. One Daimler waits in deeply sunken road at H.1. d. 5.4.
2/4 Dukes still at Bluff about A.30. d. 9.2, removing any time.
Cars run up road to ADS in H.1. c, G. 6 b, A. 30 c.
All evacuations good.

8.30 pm.
27. 8. 18.

(Signed) H.B.Pope
Major R.A.M.C.

Report No 6.

A.D.M.S. 62nd Division.

There is no change in the disposition of the R.A.Ps. Owing to the relief of 187th Inf Bde by 185th Inf Bde, the R.A.Ps of the left sector are now,

R.A.P.   1/5 Devons. } B. 28. a 4.8.
          7/20 Londons }

For the moment, however, the M.O. 7/20th Londons is at Bde Hdqrs dugout B. 13 c. 2.7.
R.A.P. 8 W.Yorks in Sunken Road at B. 15. d. 0.5.
186th Inf. Bde, unchanged.

(Signed) H.B.Pope.
Major R.A.M.C.

4 pm
28. 8. 18

Report No. 7

ADMS 62nd Division.

Evacuation of 185th Inf. Bde unchanged.
RaP. 8th W/York. B.15.d.0.5 carrying to quarry at B.14.a.4.4. thence by Ford to ADS.
RaP. 1/5 Devons }
     2/20 London } B.28.a.4.6.
thence by Ford car or bearers to Lone Tree relay (now 185th Inf Bde Hdqrs) at B27.c.7.8, thence by Ford or Daimler to Water Point on Main Road B.26.a.1.8 & by Daimler to ADS.
The GOC. 185 Inf. Bde has been approached & a squad together with stores can be left in the dug out.

Evacuation of 186th Inf. Bde.
   2/4 Dukes. H.4.a.4.8.
   5th Dukes. H.4.c.3.5. in willow hedge.
   2/4 Hants. Not in action.
Evacuation as above. Ford cars can get to both RaPs.

(Signed) H B Pope
Major RAMC

30. 8. 18.
9. 30 pm.

Report No. 8

ADMS. 62nd Div.

Evacuations remain as yesterday.
Positions of RaPs unaltered.
It is proposed to relieve the 186th Inf Bde by the 187th Inf Bde, tonight.

(Signed) H B Pope.
Major RAMC

31. 8. 18.
9 pm.

Report No. 9

ADMS. 62nd Division.

The position of RaPs is unchanged, Daimler cars run to the Ervillers – Sapignies Road from the ADS by 3 routes, Gomiecourt – Ervillers: Gomiecourt to light railway X where a Bearer Post is situated B.26.a.1.8. & Gomiecourt Behagnies. Cars can also run along the Main Road & connect up the three loading Posts.
Ford Cars can run to the Relay Post in the sunken road at B.27.c.7.8. & have made an advanced dump of stretchers & stores here tonight, they run across country no road being available, using the old German track to VAUX. Owing to information concerning traffic routes being received this morning that the road Gomiecourt – Ervillers is a single route in the direction of Ervillers only, a walking wounded collecting post has been established at the Loading Post B. 13. d. 1. 5. The YMCA are going to assist.

8-45 pm.
29. 8. 18.

(Signed) H B Pope.
Major RAMC

MEDICAL

Army Form C. 2118.

WAR DIARY
or
INTELLIGENCE SUMMARY.
(Erase heading not required.)

Summary of Events and Information

War Diary
of
2/1st West Riding Field Ambulance.

PERIOD 1st – 30th SEP./1918.

Volume XXI

CONFIDENTIAL.

MEDICAL

Army Form C. 2118.

WAR DIARY
or
INTELLIGENCE SUMMARY.
(Erase heading not required.)

Instructions regarding War Diaries and Intelligence Summaries are contained in F. S. Regs., Part II. and the Staff Manual respectively. Title pages will be prepared in manuscript.

Place	Date	Hour	Summary of Events and Information	Remarks and references to Appendices
Hospital S.T.P. Mvy y AYETTE	September 1st		Trops lines F.11. c. 4.9 ADS. H.1.b.6.7 (A.D.S. ŚEHAGNIES) Capt. J.M. Pritch awarded the Cwt. (A/Maj) Hirst awarded D.C.M. (Mys 931/8/15) (Anderson BR.)	AW/SR
			62 Br. Atone ads returning began him to be moved to SEHAGNIES. Received 1st Lieut. GWYNN. A.R.C. USA detached an No 1/c. 8" Field Ambs during absence of Medical Officers on leave to UK.	ADMS
SÉHAGNIES H.1.b.6.7 (WATERLOT FARM)	2nd		Major Hirst began to SEHAGNIES, arrived 3.20 pm. 62nd Br. Atone ads M. 54 Received. Wounded evacuated through ADS MDS from Bri.	ADR
	4		1 Lieut. R.J. St. Louis detailed as No 1/c. 62nd Br Machine Gun Battalion during absence New No 1/c to leave to U.K. (ADMS M/520/10). Mary etc F 2 (French) General Reserve down in front Arrowleg DAPPING. Specimens of Germans A.F.S. etc forwarded to Army Medical Museum. War in Paris. Undated Le Jan a divisional restoration. Pit Cholera	AW AW/PRES
	5th		work on ADS Commenced (Chart 5/c. H.i.b.6.5. (Plan attached	
	9th		20 French men 18th Inf Ah attached as additional stretcher bearers (ADMS M.29 A9/9/16) 1 Lieut Penny A.R.C. USA relieved 1 Lieut Gwynn on leave No 16 Stockyards during 14 C.M. was Killed.	BAO
			62 A.C. Ashore order No 555 issued — move detayed 24 hours	

D. D. & L., London, E.C. (A8091) Wt. W1771/M2931 750,000 5/17 Sch. 52 Forms C2118/14

Army Form C. 2118.

WAR DIARY
or
INTELLIGENCE SUMMARY.
(Erase heading not required.)

Instructions regarding War Diaries and Intelligence Summaries are contained in F. S. Regs., Part II. and the Staff Manual respectively. Title pages will be prepared in manuscript.

Place	Date	Hour	Summary of Events and Information	Remarks and references to Appendices
SCHAGNES WERLOT FARM H.1.6.7 Ref S7 D.	September 10th		Capt Harloge M.C. returned attached to 185 Dn/Gas Hq as Liaison Officer. Capt HoPickles O.C. 1/Queen Battalion +20 Ranks (Aunders) attached to 2/3 Toest Riding Field Ambulance. Returns for 62 Div. Administration Pub. received.	App 1
	11th		62 Bin. Medical Arrangement received. Inst. St Louis attached to Unit for duty (Appx N.772 F10/9/18.) 2 Horse ambulances T+Shore Pain Wagons attached 2/3 W.R.F Amb. (Appx N.758 F10/9/18.) 4 Gunwies, 1 Ford and 3 Pierce Squares attached 2/2 W.R.F Amb (Appx N.716/8)	App 2
	12th 15th		Capt P.J. Dibb authoriti posted to Unit as Commanding Officer (A.D.M.S m.955) 62 Bn. RAMC. orders S6 received. Arrangements made to relieve Sick of 187 Bd. the morning of 16th.	App 3 App 6
	16		Cases S.cin collected. Capt P. Dibb M.C. body returned to Unit. Capt LA Macking M.C. teen returned to Unit. Capt Gn Ginigh M.C. Senior M.Officer, Capt. Littlewhate Bds. taken on Strength (Appx BTS N.12/9/18.	App 4
	17th		Spain leave returned to their unit. Collector 185 Dy Ae Sec. Commenced	App 5
	22nd		Capt A.G. Hassermanne A.D. RAMC(TF) arrived at HqT 3/1st W.R.Gs admits for Quting	App 6

D. D. & L., London, E.C.
(A8004) Wt. W1771/M2031 750,000 5/17 Sch. 52 Forms/C2118/14

Army Form C. 2118.

WAR DIARY
or
INTELLIGENCE SUMMARY.
(Erase heading not required.)

Instructions regarding War Diaries and Intelligence Summaries are contained in F. S. Regs., Part II. and the Staff Manual respectively. Title pages will be prepared in manuscript.

Place	Date	Hour	Summary of Events and Information	Remarks and references to Appendices
BEHAGNIES Watfield-From H.1.8.67. Sheet 57D	September 23rd		Major H.B. Pope R.a.m.c. proceeded on leave	A/L
	24th		Ext- from 62nd Div a.D.m.s Inst- received 185 Inf- Bde order no 25 received 62" Div Ramc order No 57 received 186 Inf Bde order no 157 received Capt- Maclennan M.C. Ramc r 2 B.R. detailed t 185 Bde H.Q. as Liaison Officer. Two Bearer S/Beats r one runner detailed to Arch R.M.O. of 9th D.L.I. 2/20 London Rgt. 1/5 Devons, 8" W. Yorks.	A/L
	26"		Capt- H.D. Ricketts m.c Ramc writ 32 Bearers r 3 horse Ambs attached to 2/3 W.R. Fd Amb. to duty – 30 Bandsmen from 185 Bde attached to Men 2/1st W.R. Fd Amb reported direct to O.C. 2/3 W.R. Fd Amb on instructions from a.D.m.S. Three Bearers sub-sects r 1 Fnd Amb 186 Bde order no 158 received – reported to Sub- to O.C. 2/3 W.R. Fd Amb – A fatigue party of 1 N.C.O. – 7 O.R. detailed for duty to clear up B.T. (mainly of Yk. & R. at BAPAUME area) for reception of walking wounded). Ramc. order no 58 received – a.D.m.s. order no 186 Bde order no 158 received – 186 Bde order no 159 received	A/L
	27"		1st Lt- R.f. St Laur. Gn O.R.C. U.S.a. detailed for duty at F.D.S. 2/2 W.R. Fd Amb.	A/L

Army Form C. 2118.

WAR DIARY
or
INTELLIGENCE SUMMARY.
(Erase heading not required.)

Instructions regarding War Diaries and Intelligence Summaries are contained in F. S. Regs., Part II. and the Staff Manual respectively. Title pages will be prepared in manuscript.

Place	Date	Hour	Summary of Events and Information	Remarks and references to Appendices
BEHAGNIES Wancourt-Bavin H.1.b.6.7. Sheet 57D	September 27th		1st Lt Gwynn M.ORC. U.S.A. was detailed to report to A&Q and 2nd Lieut for temporary duty — Ame C.S. Wagon was detailed to report to OC 62nd Div. Recp Stn escort for the purpose of drawing rations. Capt E.M. Ashcroft Reime reported to this unit for duty from the 62nd Div R.S.	A.H/s

A. Helmhurst
Lt. Col
Reune

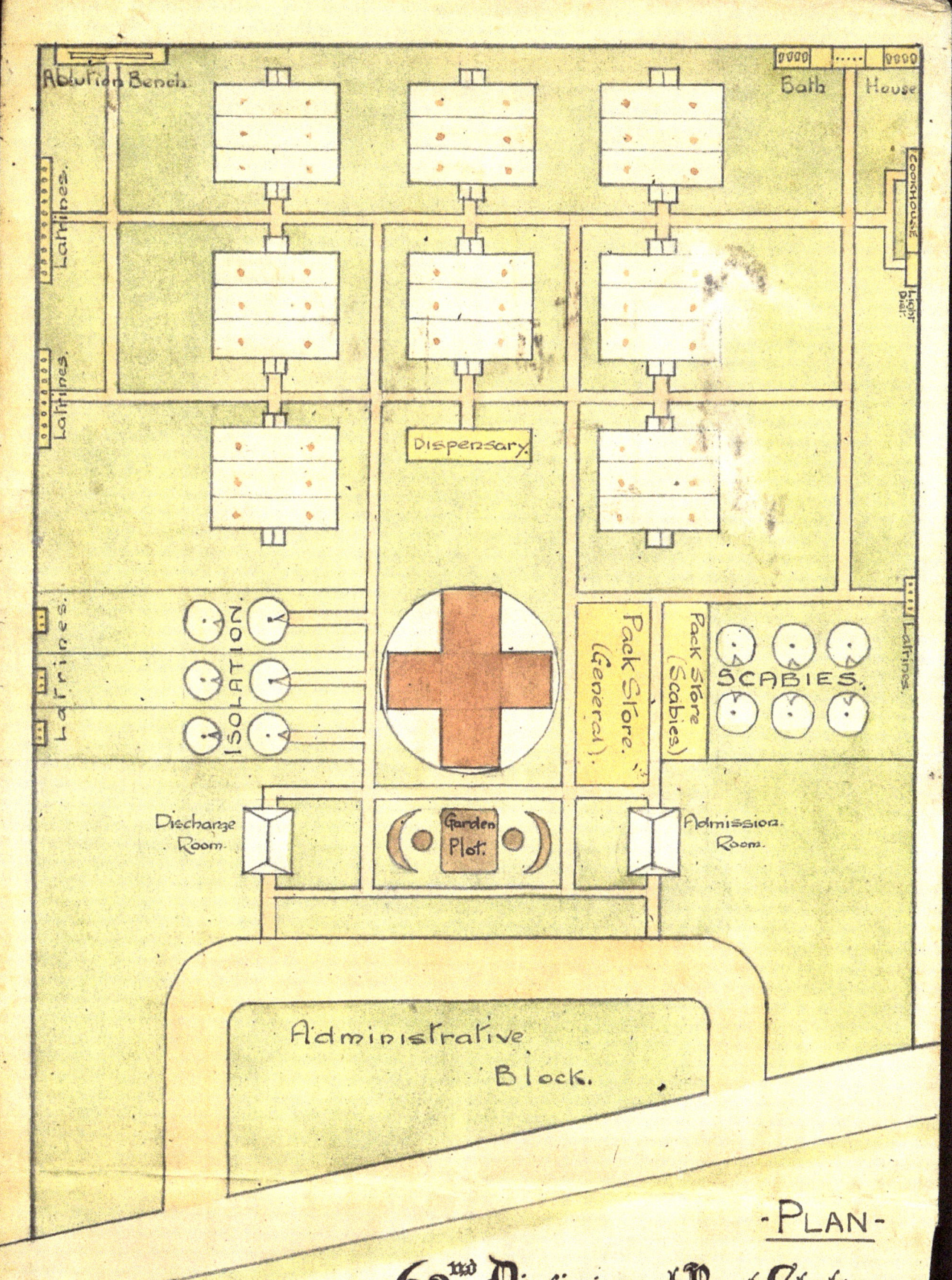

- PLAN -

62ⁿᵈ Divisional Rest Station.

(2/1st W. R. Field Ambce).

Army Form C. 2118.

WAR DIARY
or
INTELLIGENCE SUMMARY.

(*Erase heading not required.*)

Instructions regarding War Diaries and Intelligence Summaries are contained in F. S. Regs., Part II. and the Staff Manual respectively. Title pages will be prepared in manuscript.

Place	Date	Hour	Summary of Events and Information	Remarks and references to Appendices

(A8001) Wt. W1771/M2931 750,000 5/17 D. D. & L., London, E.C. Sch. 53 Forms/C2118/14

MEDICAL

Army Form C. 2118.
Original

WAR DIARY
or
INTELLIGENCE SUMMARY.
(Erase heading not required.)

ORIGINAL

- CONFIDENTIAL -

WAR DIARY

- of -

2/1st West Riding Field Ambulance.

Period 1st to 30th Oct/1918.

Volume XXII.

Army Form C. 2118.

WAR DIARY
or
INTELLIGENCE SUMMARY.

(Erase heading not required.)

Original

Place	Date	Hour	Summary of Events and Information	Remarks and references to Appendices
BEHAGNIES Sheet 57C Baillulet Farm H.2.6.7	1918 Oct 1st		Capt. Mackenzie M.C. returned with Q of 2/1 W.R.F. Amb. from duty as Gasan Officer with 185 Bde. 1st Lt. St. Louis returned to H.Q. of 2/1 W.R.F. Amb. from duty with 2/2 W.R.F. Amb. on D.S.	Aff
	Oct 2nd		62nd Div. Route order to be received - A holding party was detailed to proceed to BEAUMETZ LES CAMBRAI for the new D.R.S. 15th Group Units	Aff
	Oct 3rd		Lt. Col. A.G. Hollinrake O.C. and Captn. Azzopita with Major Blackburn M.C. and Capt. Ashcroft proceed to BEAUMETZ LES CAMBRAI to arrange the site for new D.R.S. - Capt. Ashcroft remained at the new site which was to be open on Oct 4th at 8 a.m.	Aff
	Oct 4th		The 2/1st W.R.F. Amb. moved to the new D.R.S. located J.13.B.4.2. The Sheet 57C. - This site had previously been a German C.C.S. The accommodation for sick is in wooden huts, left intact - an excellent hutch built. Cook house remains not accommodation available for 200 patients. Lt. D'Huris called during the afternoon at the D.R.S. - 1st Lt. C.T. Searcy M.O.R.C. U.S.A. is struck off the strength of the unit, having been posted as M.O. to B. W. York Bn.	Aff

Army Form C. 2118.

WAR DIARY
or
INTELLIGENCE SUMMARY.
(Erase heading not required.)

Original

Instructions regarding War Diaries and Intelligence Summaries are contained in F.S. Regs., Part II. and the Staff Manual respectively. Title pages will be prepared in manuscript.

Place	Date	Hour	Summary of Events and Information	Remarks and references to Appendices
BEAUMETZ LES CAMBRAI I.13.b.4.2 Sheet 57C	1918 Oct 5th		Capt. Ashcroft was detached on Duty to 62nd Div. R.B.	Afk
	Oct 7th	6a.m.	1st Lt. G.H. Gwynn is struck off the strength & posted to 2nd Div. authority Third Army No 3046/1/48A of 22/9/18	Afk
	Oct 8th		62 (WR) Div RAMC order No 61 received. Also 183 Bde order No 30	Afk
			62 (WR) Div RAMC order No 62 received	
	Oct 9th		The DMS at BEAUMETZ was transferred over to 8th Div. and 3rd Div – The 2/1 WR Fd Amb moved to HAVRINCOURT.	Afk
HAVRINCOURT 6.c.10. K.33.b.6.5 Sheet 57C	Oct 10th		1 N.C.O + 10 men were sent to the E.M.O. at HAVRINCOURT. The 2/1st WR Fd Amb moved to MARCOING Major Pope returned from leave - Watts Knighton	Afk
MARCOING Oct 11th L.22.b.0.5 Sheet 57C	Oct 11th		185 Inf Bde order No 31 received – 2/1st WR Fd Amb moved from MARCOING to CATTENIERES where 15 Bearers officer Capt Pickles M.C. + Bearers rejoined from 2/2 WR Fd Amb	Afk

D. D. & L., London, E.C.
(A800) Wt. W1771/M2091 75v,000 5/7 Sch. 52 Forms/C2118/14

Army Form C. 2118.

Original

WAR DIARY
or
INTELLIGENCE SUMMARY.
(Erase heading not required.)

Instructions regarding War Diaries and Intelligence Summaries are contained in F. S. Regs., Part II. and the Staff Manual respectively. Title pages will be prepared in manuscript.

Place	Date	Hour	Summary of Events and Information	Remarks and references to Appendices
CATENIERES H.12.a.7.2 Sheet 57 B.	1918 Oct 12th		All the water supplies of this village were tested for impurities & report sent to 185 Inf Bde H.Q. - Wells were marked when fit for use and amount of B.P. required per diem were noted. — General carcases of horses were removed from stables & yards and burnt.	AHc
	Oct 13th		62 (W.R.) Div Ramc relieved 2/1 W.R. Div Ambce moves from CATTENIERES to BEVILLERS.	AHc
BEVILLERS C.29.a.2.8 Sheet 57 B.	Oct 14th		All the water supplies of this village were tested for impurity & report sent to 185 Bde HQ - Wells were marked when fit for use & amount of B.P. required per diem were noted.	AHc
	Oct 15th		Capt H.S. Pickles M.C. was detailed for camp duty as M.O. to 2/4 KOYLI. 2 Ambces were detailed to 2/2 CWTR Div Amb -	AHc
	Oct 16th		Major Blackburn M.C. proceeds on leave to U.K. - 62 (W.R.) Div Renn orders No 62 received	AHc

D. D. & L., London, E.C.
(A8001) Wt. W1777/M2431 750,000 5/17 Sch. 52 Forms/C2118/14

Army Form C. 2118.

Original

WAR DIARY
or
INTELLIGENCE SUMMARY.
(Erase heading not required.)

Instructions regarding War Diaries and Intelligence Summaries are contained in F. S. Regs., Part II. and the Staff Manual respectively. Title pages will be prepared in manuscript.

Place	Date	Hour	Summary of Events and Information	Remarks and references to Appendicies
BEVILLERS C.29.a.2.8 Sht 57B	1918 Oct 17th		Amendment to 62(WR)Div Reun C order no 64 received — 10 Rein/member arrived from 16 Bam for July — 1st Dr A.S. Robinson on NR & USa reported for duty & in taken on the strength of the unit — 3 Daimler motor Ambs were loaned to OC 2/2 WR 9F Amb for evacuation purposes.	Appx
	Oct 18th		The motor ambs returned from 2/2 W.R. 9F Amb.	Appx
	Oct 19th		15 men from 2/20 London Reg & 15 fm 8 W.Yorks reported as bearers to the unit. 62(WR) Div Reun order no 65 received. 185 Bde orders no 33 & 34 received. — Capt G.A Mackenzie R.A.C. – 3 N.COs & 18 Sprs & OR other bearers together with the 30 above noted bearers proceeded to H.Q. of 2/2 W.R. 9F Amb for duty in forward area — The 3 Horse Ambs and 4 Motor ambs (Daimler) also reported for duty to OC 2/2 WR 9F Amb.	Appx
	Oct 21st		4 our Reune towards 1 the unit reported wounded in action.	Appx
	Oct 22nd		62nd Div Reune order no 66 received.	Appx

Army Form C. 2118.

Original

WAR DIARY
or
INTELLIGENCE SUMMARY.
(Erase heading not required.)

Place	Date	Hour	Summary of Events and Information	Remarks and references to Appendices
BEVILLERS O.29.a.2.8 Sheet 57B	1918 Oct 23.		Personnel from forward area returned to H.Q. Ambulances also returned to H.Q.	
	-28th		2nd Lieut Robinson MORC USA was detailed for Temporary duty 6.2/3rd W=R Fd Amb.	A/Sh
	-29th		62nd Div R.A.M.C. order No 67 received.	A/Sh
	-30		Orders received from 186 Bde for Nos 2/1 WR Hand to move to BOLESMES under orders of G.O.C 186.Bde. One Officer proceeded to arrange billets in advance (Applemore)	A/Sh
	-31st		The unit moved at 0750 to BOLESMES via St HILAIRE St VAAST, St PYTHON, arriving at 1130 – The sick of 186 & 187 Bdes will be collected by this unit.	A/Sh

A.J. McWilliam
Lt-Col
OC 2/1 WR Fd Amb

"MEDICAL"

Army Form C. 2118.

Original

WAR DIARY
or
INTELLIGENCE SUMMARY.
(Erase heading not required.)

Summary of Events and Information

Confidential

ORIGINAL

WAR DIARY

of

2/1st West Riding F'd Amb-

Period 1st to 30th Nov/18.

Volume XXIII

MEDICAL
Army Form C. 2118.
Original

WAR DIARY
or
INTELLIGENCE SUMMARY.
(Erase heading not required.)

Place	Date	Hour	Summary of Events and Information	Remarks and references to Appendices
	1918			
SOLESMES	Nov 1st		62nd Div RAMC order 68 received - Capt Lawson proceeded to ROMERIES harassing with-for this unit. Three NCOs & 40 men were sent to C.C.S. on SOLESMES - St PYTHON road to assist in establishing same - Lt AE Rahman MORC USA was detailed for temporary duty with 2/4 KOYLI Bn. -	A/L
	Nov 2nd		The NCOs & men returned from C.C.S. on SOLESMES - St PYTHON road. One NCO 2 squads of bearers & 1 runner was detailed to each Bn of 187 Inf Bde Group - The unit moves to ROMERIES.	A/L A/L
ROMERIES	Nov 3rd		Major Blackburn MC. returned from leave	A/L
	Nov 4th	5pm	The unit moves to ESCARMAIN. - 90 men reported to this unit for duty. as extra bearers from the three Inf Bns.	A/L
ESCARMAIN	" 6th		The unit moves to ORSINVAL after resting at RUESNES. - Capt O'Sullivan RAMC reported for duty & was taken on its strength.	A/L
ORSINVAL	" 7th		The unit moves to GOMMEGNIES. - 62nd Div order no 71 received - an Int-subdivision reported at M.D.S. for duty from 2/3 WR FA Amb. - Lt Grossman MORC was attached for duty from 2/2 WR D Amb. M.D.S. opened at 10 am - Instructions received to admit convoys from French Div.	A/L A/L

T2134. Wt. W708—776. 500000. 4/15. Sir J. C. & 8.

Army Form C. 2118.

Original

WAR DIARY
or
INTELLIGENCE SUMMARY.
(Erase heading not required.)

Instructions regarding War Diaries and Intelligence Summaries are contained in F.S. Regs., Part II. and the Staff Manual respectively. Title pages will be prepared in manuscript.

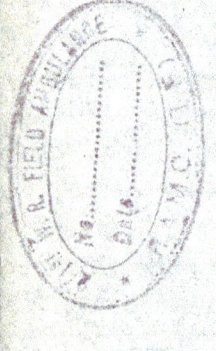

Place	Date	Hour	Summary of Events and Information	Remarks and references to Appendices
	1918			
GOMMEGNIES	Nov 9th		The unit moved to QUENE au LOUP.	A/tk
"	-10th		The unit moved to SOUS-LE-BOIS where a M.D.S. & D.R.S. was opened in the Hospice.	A/tk
"	-11th		Armistice was declared at 11 a.m.	A/tk
"	-12th		Orders were received for move of the Division to the German Frontier. The O.C. 2/1 W.R. O/Comd proceeded on leave to England.	A/tk
SOUS LE BOIS	-15		Handed over D.R.S. & M.D.S. to the 2/3rd West Riding Field Ambulance at 2000 hours	D/A/tk
"	-16		Moved to FERRIERE LE GRAND.	D/A/tk
FERRIERE LE GRD	-18		Moved to MONTIGNIES ST. CHRISTOPHE.	D/A/tk
MONTIGNIES	-19		Moved to MARBAIX.	D/A/tk
MARBAIX	-20		Moved to FROMIÉE.	D/A/tk
FROMIÉE	-21		Party Rein. W/OC mobile medical unit for SPA.	D/A/tk
"	"		Moved to METTET.	D/A/tk
METTET	-25		Moved to WARNANT.	D/A/tk
WARNANT	-26		Moved to SENENNE. OC returned from leave.	D/A/tk
SENENNE	-27th		The unit moved to CHAPOIS.	A/tk
CHAPOIS	-28th		The 62nd Div has to-day been transferred to IX Corps. The detachment with Mobile Medical unit returned to 1HQ.	A/tk FIELD AMBULANCE

Army Form C. 2118.

Original

WAR DIARY
or
INTELLIGENCE SUMMARY.
(Erase heading not required.)

Instructions regarding War Diaries and Intelligence Summaries are contained in F. S. Regs., Part II. and the Staff Manual respectively. Title pages will be prepared in manuscript.

Place	Date	Hour	Summary of Events and Information	Remarks and references to Appendices

ORIGINAL "62 DIV" BOX 2934

MEDICAL Army Form C. 2118.

WAR DIARY
or
INTELLIGENCE SUMMARY.
(Erase heading not required.)

Vol 2
WO 95/81

— Confidential —

WAR DIARY

of

2/1st West Riding Field Ambulance.

Period. 1/31 Dec. 1918.

Volume XXIV.

COMMITTEE FOR THE
MEDICAL HISTORY OF THE WAR
6 MAR 1919

Army Form C. 2118.

WAR DIARY
or
INTELLIGENCE SUMMARY.

(Erase heading not required.)

Place	Date	Hour	Summary of Events and Information	Remarks and references to Appendices
CHAPOIS	1918 Dec 6		Unit moves to SCY. Capt Mackenzie struck off strength	a/h
SCY	- 10		- - - CHARDENEUX	a/h
CHARDENEUX	- 11		- - - HAMOIR	a/h
HAMOIR	- 12		- - - HABIEMONT	a/h
HABIEMONT	- 13		- - - GRAND HALLEUX	a/h
Gd. HALLEUX	- 14		- - - RENCHEUX	a/h
RENCHEUX	- 15		Lt Lupton MORE USA taken on strength	a/h
-	- 16		Unit moves to AMEL (GERMANY) - Crossed frontier at 1045 hrs -	a/h
AMEL	- 17		- - - BERG.	a/h
BERG	- 20		Capt Pickles M.C. struck off strength -	a/h
-	- 21		Unit moves to REMSCHEID	a/h
REMSCHEID	- 22		- - - HELLENTHAL.	a/h
HELLENTHAL	- 23		- - - STREMPT.	a/h
STREMPT	- 24		- - - GEHN.	a/h
GEHN	- 29		Hospital opened at KOMMERN in Civilian Hospital - accom to beds	a/h
-	- 31		Unit moves to final destination at GLEHN.	a/h

A. Hebblethwaite
Lt W.D. Field Ambulance

MEDICAL

Army Form C. 2118.

WAR DIARY
or
INTELLIGENCE SUMMARY.
(Erase heading not required.)

- CONFIDENTIAL -

WAR DIARY
- of -

2/1st West Riding Field Ambce.

Period:-
1st Jany 1919 to 31st Jany/19.

Volume XXV

ORIGINAL

Jany 19.

MEDICAL

Army Form C. 2118.

Original

WAR DIARY
or
INTELLIGENCE SUMMARY.
(Erase heading not required.)

Army Form C. 2118.

Instructions regarding War Diaries and Intelligence Summaries are contained in F. S. Regs., Part II. and the Staff Manual respectively. Title pages will be prepared in manuscript.

ORIGINAL

Place	Date	Hour	Summary of Events and Information	Remarks and references to Appendices
GLEHN	1919 Jan 1st		The arrivals of the unit were inspected by 62 Gen DADVS.	Appx
	2nd		Lt A. E. Robinson M.O.R.C. USA was detailed for temporary duty as M.O. to 9th D.A.S.	Appx
	6th		Our N.C.O.'s and orderly own details to proceed to T Corps H.Q. (2 D.Sub) for temporary duty in venereal work — off	Appx
	9th		The hospital at Kommern was inspected by the 2 D.Sub T Corps & ADMS 62 w Div	Appx
	14th		Capt W. B. Lawson proceeded on leave to England. His duties being taken over in the interim by Major Blackburn M.O.	Appx
	19th		The 2 DMS 2 w Army inspected the troops at Kommern with T Corps 2 D.Sub & 62 w Div ADMS	Appx
	20th		The following awards are notified by 1st & 5th French Army: Croix de Guerre (Gold Star) to Capt (A'man) H.B. Pope, Croix de Guerre (Silver Star) to Dvr I.D. Clark M.T ASC	Appx

Army Form C. 2118.

Original

WAR DIARY
or
~~INTELLIGENCE SUMMARY.~~

(Erase heading not required.)

Instructions regarding War Diaries and Intelligence Summaries are contained in F. S. Regs., Part II. and the Staff Manual respectively. Title pages will be prepared in manuscript.

Place	Date	Hour	Summary of Events and Information	Remarks and references to Appendices
GHEHM	1919 Jan 21st		Capt O'Sullivan was detailed for temporary duty with	
			5th K.O.Y.L.I. as M.O.	
			Capt. G.W. Rea R.AMC reported to this unit for duty	A/P/L
			Lt. Triplett M.O.R.C U.S.A. is struck off strength of this unit	A/P/L
	23rd			
	28th		(A/Major) Capt- H.P. Pope was awarded M.C.	
			The following on mentions in despatches	
			2nd Lt Newbury W.C. and Pte Evans L	
			Sgt. Wood J.D. was awarded M.S.M.	
	30th		O/C 22nd IX Corps inspected this Hosp. at Kon menen	A/P/L
	31st		A Conference of C.O. was held at 185 R.st Hosp	A/P/L

MEDICAL

Army Form C. 2118.

140/3024
Original

2/1st W.R.
FIELD AMBULANCE,
R.A.M.C. (T.F.)
No. ....
Date ....

WAR DIARY
or
INTELLIGENCE SUMMARY.
(Erase heading not required.)

CONFIDENTIAL.

WAR DIARY

OF

2/1 WEST RIDING FIELD AMBULANCE.

FROM 1st FEB 1919 TO 28th FEB 1919

VOLUME XXV

Army Form C. 2118.

2/1st W.R.
FIELD AMBULANCE,
R.A.M.C. (T.F.)

No. ....
Date ....

WAR DIARY
or
INTELLIGENCE SUMMARY.
(Erase heading not required.)

Instructions regarding War Diaries and Intelligence Summaries are contained in F. S. Regs., Part II. and the Staff Manual respectively. Title pages will be prepared in manuscript.

Original

Place	Date	Hour	Summary of Events and Information	Remarks and references to Appendices
GLEHN.	Feb 1st 1919		Lt. Col. A.C. Hebblethwaite left for leave to PARIS.	fol 13
	- 2nd		Fire occurred in billet No 43 in this village.	fol 13
	- 3rd		A court of Inquiry was held in respect of the fire above mentioned - with president Major Blackburn + members Capt. Rea + Lt. Robinson.	fol 13
			A case of diphtheria has to-day been notified in the civil population of this village.	fol 13
	- 4th		A conference of Educational Officers took place at 185 Bde H.Q.	fol 13
	- 5th		185 Bde Orders No 22 received.	fol 13
	- 6th		Surplus horses under the new Establishment were handed over as follows:	fol 13
			2 Riders to 8th W. Yorks	
			1 - - 2/20 London Regt.	
			1 Lt. Draft - 312 Bde R.F.A.	
			3 - - mules 9th D.L.I.	
			2 L.D. horses to 62nd Div Train.	
	- 10th		Lt. Col. A.C. Hebblethwaite returned from Paris leave.	fol 13
			Four O.R. proceeded to 64 C.C.S. for venereal prophylactic work.	fol 13
	- 11th		Pte H. Robinson proceeds on leave to U.K.	fol 13

Army Form C. 2118.

2/1ST W.R.
FIELD AMBULANCE,
R.A.M.C. (T.F.)

No.
Date

WAR DIARY
or
INTELLIGENCE SUMMARY

(Erase heading not required.)

Instructions regarding War Diaries and Intelligence Summaries are contained in F. S. Regs., Part II. and the Staff Manual respectively. Title pages will be prepared in manuscript.

Place	Date	Hour	Summary of Events and Information	Remarks and references to Appendices
GLEHN	Feb 13th 1919	—	March tables for 185 O.B.C. (O.H.M.) No 22 received	appx
	14th	—	8. S/Sgt Hensley W. promoted Acting Sergeants from 8/12/18 — Q.M.S. 8/11/19	
			Sergt Wood J.D. — — Q.M.S. 8/11/19	
			— Blackborough T — — S/Sgt 8/12/18	
			— Knaggs H. — — S/Sgt 17/1/19	
			One G.S. wagon, one water-cart, one horse ambulance wagon	appx
	15th	—	handed over to R.T.O Mechernich as surplus under new Field Ambulance Equipment.	
			The A.D.M.S. gave an address to 1/5 Yorks on Demobilisation —	appx
	17th	—	Notification that B.A.B. code had fallen into enemy hands. all copies in the W. Stream from units.	appx
	20th	—	Major Pope M.C. v P/L Pickering Rene. proceed to Euskirchen to attend a Court Martial.	appx
	21st	—	Capt (a/Major) J. H. Blackburn relinquishes his acting rank on allens establishment of Field Ambulance	appx

Army Form C. 2118.

WAR DIARY
or
INTELLIGENCE SUMMARY.
(Erase heading not required.)

Place	Date	Hour	Summary of Events and Information	Remarks and references to Appendices
GLEHN	Feb 26th 1919		The following promotions have been confirmed—	
			S/Sgt. Gill H to be Acting Sergt. from 8/1/19	
			Corp Richardson H — — — — — 8/12/18	
			— Spedding A.E. — — — — — 2/1/19	

A.J. Wilmrath
Lt-Col
Officer Commanding
2/1st W.R. Field Ambulance.

WAR DIARY
or
INTELLIGENCE SUMMARY

2/1st W.R.
FIELD A. BULANCE.
R.A.M.C. 2nd T.F.

WO/27
140/3551

Confidential
War Diary
of
2/1 West Riding Field Ambulance

From 1st March 1919 to 31st March 1919

Volume XXVI

WAR DIARY
or
INTELLIGENCE SUMMARY.
(Erase heading not required.)

Army _____

Place	Date	Hour	Summary of Events and Information	Remarks and references to Appendices
GLEHN	March 4 1919		Authority to promote 40140 Pte Drake N. and No 401276 Pte Jake H. to rank of Sgt as instructors to the Unit received -	AJE
		2.0	2.S/Sgt Blatchford's rank confirmed as substantive - authority o/c RAMC records 59/1686/372	AJE
		4.0	RAMC other ranks received (move of 187 Bde to new area)	AJE
		5.0	Surplus lendered G.S. wagon handed over to Ordnance Officer MECHERNICH	AJE
		8.0	RAMC other ranks No 82 received (move of 186 Bde to new area)	AJE
		9.0	Capt O'Sullivan P.J. proceeds to 74th Bde R.F.A. as M.O.	AJE
		10.0	Capt G. Sullivan M.J. returned to the Unit.	AJE
		12.0	RAMC other ranks No 83 received (move of 185 Bde to new area)	AJE

WAR DIARY
or
INTELLIGENCE SUMMARY.
(Erase heading not required.)

Army Form C.2118.

2/1st W.O. FIELD AMBULANCE R.A.M.C.

Original

Place	Date	Hour	Summary of Events and Information	Remarks and references to Appendices
GLEHN	March 13 1919		185 Inf. Bde. Group order No. 24 received (2/1 WR 91 Amb. to move to MÖLLERSHEIM on 14/3)	A.1/4
			Lt-Col. A. McIllwraith proceeded to Duisburg on 13 April's notice to Me. for to command.	A.1/4 A.1/4
MÖLLERSHEIM	Feby 14 1919		Unit arrived at MÖLLERSHEIM. front road.	
	Mar 15		Major J. Bevis assumed charge of "England" Division.	
	"		authority to dissolve received by Maj the Camps. Heavburn letters on Rhine	
	Mar 16		Capt. W.T.E. Batcher proceeded to Army today to Area commandant In dept.	
	Mar 17		Capt. J.W.O. Stivers proceeded to Army today to Area commandant In dept.	
			Capt. D.E. Ryan A.O.C. U.S.A proceeded to take medical charge Mar Rhine	
			Col. A.J. Blunt M. Bunn M.E.	
			Capt. Gun. Rea. from No.1 to the R.A.A. taken on Strength.	
	Mar 19		Majors H. Blair (who is speaker at Aerodrome) and J. Hayes on proceeding to No 2 Concentration Camp Dunnish to antiquities. Ed. Lge. Wakham also proceeded to Devon for demobilization took over the command of the unit	
			today Brierly Rhine appear to by the band was taken to the strength from this date	Full

WAR DIARY
or
INTELLIGENCE SUMMARY.
(Erase heading not required.)

Army Form C. 2118. T. Fd.

2/1st W.R. FIELD AMBULANCE.

Original

Place	Date	Hour	Summary of Events and Information	Remarks and references to Appendices
MOLLERSHEIM	Mar 22		Lieut HG E Stanyford proceeded to the 10th Ar SH for duty and was struck off the strength from the date	
	Mar 23		Hors Cmdr then sent motorcyclist 227½/3 3rd Fund	
	24		74 Gen on 75/023258 Pte J A Gannon and 403635 Pte J W Toulinson for Militery fair	Sent
	27		A.D.M.S. Inspection all rounds	Sent
	28		Sentences to Pte Toulinson and Pte Gannon promulgated. Pte Gannon sentenced to 14 days FP No 2 + forfeits 35 days pay. Pte Toulinson to 14 days FP No 2 + forfeits 28 days pay, both were sent to 6th Army Detention Barracks Bologne. Welfare Scheme for Class "A" Personnel as eligible for full Bonus from 1st Feb 1919. Same instructions received with regard to NCOs & other attached Ranks	Sent Sent
	31		Nothing to report	Sent

O/c 2/1st W.R. Field Ambulance

2/1st W.R. FIELD AMBULANCE.

Original

Medical

Army Form C. 2118.

2/1st W.R. FIELD AMBULANCE, R.A.M.C. (T.F.)

No. ....
Bn. ....

WAR DIARY
or
INTELLIGENCE SUMMARY.
(Erase heading not required.)

Instructions regarding War Diaries and Intelligence Summaries are contained in F. S. Regs., Part II. and the Staff Manual respectively. Title pages will be prepared in manuscript.

Confidential

War Diary

of

2/1st West Riding Field Ambulance R.A.M.C.T.

Period 1st to 30th April 1919

Volume XXVII

Place	Date	Hour	Summary of Events and Information	Remarks and references to Appendices

Medical

Army Form C. 2118.

Original

2/1st W.R.
FIELD AMBULANCE,
R.A.M.C. (T.F.).

No. ....
Date ....

WAR DIARY

INTELLIGENCE SUMMARY.
(Erase heading not required.)

Instructions regarding War Diaries and Intelligence Summaries are contained in F. S. Regs., Part II. and the Staff Manual respectively. Title pages will be prepared in manuscript.

Place	Date	Hour	Summary of Events and Information	Remarks and references to Appendices
WOLLERSHEIM	April 4/5 1919		185th Inf Bde Order No 28 received re move of Battalions. Lt Col A. Stevenstowart resumes (return from S.in.V.D.) on arrival of the new A.D.M.S. (Col Kelly) Capt P. J. O'Sullivan proceeds on leave to U.K.	Afh
	5/4		Advice received of arrival of 52nd & 53rd Garrison Btns (Young Soldiers Battalions) to join Highland Division - these must be referenced to for medical arrangements.	Afh
	6/4		185 Inf Bde Group Order No 29 received re move of 9th Sherwoods & 8th Bk Watch -	Afh
	10/4		8th W Yorks Btn (Cadre) left the area for U.K. - Capt Scurry MORC USA (late m.o. to 8th W.Yk) reported return unit awaiting instructions from A.D.M.S.	Afh

Army Form C. 2118.

2/1st W.R.
FIELD AMBULANCE,
R.A.M.C. (T.F.)

No. ....
Date ....

Original

WAR DIARY
or
INTELLIGENCE SUMMARY.
(Erase heading not required.)

Instructions regarding War Diaries and Intelligence Summaries are contained in F.S. Regs., Part II. and the Staff Manual respectively. Title pages will be prepared in manuscript.

Place	Date	Hour	Summary of Events and Information	Remarks and references to Appendices
WOLLERSHEIM	April 11 1919		4 A. Corp. wire received (via ADMS) calling for R.A.M.C. other ranks for Special Mobilisation to proceed to Aldershot. 1 O.R. submitted from this unit.	AKR
			Capt. Scurry M.O.R.C. USA departed having been posted as M.O. to 5th Camerons	AKR
			The A.D.M.S. visited the unit.	
do	April 14		Lt.Col. Hellethwait D.S.O. proceeded on leave to U.K. ADMS visited the unit & addressed the men on demobilisation	Jones
do	do	13	New designation of 1/8 Bn. Bde. to 1st Highland Bde.	Jones
		19	Instructions from 1st Highland Bde that "Pelican" sign must be removed from Notice Board.	Jones
do	do	22	Capt. P.G. O'Sullivan returned from leave	Jones
do	do	23	Capt. O'Sullivan proceed to MR. H.E.O.Y. for duty.	Jones

D. D. & L., London, E.C.
(AF004) Wt. W1771/M2931 750,000 5/17 Sch. 52 Forms/C.2118/14

Army Form C. 2118.

2/1st W.R.
FIELD AMBULANCE,
R.A.M.C. (T.F.)

Original

WAR DIARY
or
INTELLIGENCE SUMMARY.
(Erase heading not required.)

Instructions regarding War Diaries and Intelligence Summaries are contained in F.S. Regs., Part II. and the Staff Manual respectively. Title pages will be prepared in manuscript.

Place	Date	Hour	Summary of Events and Information	Remarks and references to Appendices
WOLLERSHEIM	April 23rd /19		Attended conference at beegree of all Unit Commanders R.A.M.C. in Rhine Army	JWR
do	" 24"		Visit of Div. H.R. for inspection of Demobilization Roster by AD/M.S.	JWR
do	25		Instructions recd. to attach over medical charge of 5th Cameronians until the arrival of Capt. T.G.J. Hensley R.A.M.C	JWR
do	28		Instructions received to take over medical charge of 52 Location in the absence of Lieut. E.B. Verney R.A.M.C	JWR
do	30		Arrival of 9 R.A.M.C Reinforcements D.R.O. 74 received authorising the wearing of unit distinguishing badges. Lieut.Col A.G. Hebblethwaite O.S.O. returned from leave.	JWR

A.J.Whitworth
Lt.Colonel. T.
2/1ST W.R. FIELD AMBULANCE.

Medical

Original

Army Form C. 2118.

WAR DIARY
or
INTELLIGENCE SUMMARY.
(Erase heading not required.)

Instructions regarding War Diaries and Intelligence Summaries are contained in F. S. Regs., Part II. and the Staff Manual respectively. Title pages will be prepared in manuscript.

CONFIDENTIAL

WAR DIARY

of

2/1 WEST RIDING FIELD AMBULANCE

From 1st May 1919 To 31st May 1919

VOLUME XXVIII

Medical.

Army Form C. 2118.

WAR DIARY
or
INTELLIGENCE SUMMARY.
(Erase heading not required.)

Instructions regarding War Diaries and Intelligence
Summaries are contained in F. S. Regs., Part II.
and the Staff Manual respectively. Title pages
will be prepared in manuscript.

Place	Date	Hour	Summary of Events and Information	Remarks and references to Appendices
	1919			
WOLLERSHEIM	May 2		The commanding officer attended a Conference at office of ADMS	
"	-	4	Eight RAMC reinforcements to the unit arrived	
"	-	7	The C.O. visited HEIMBACH in regards to billets for the unit	
"	-	8	1st Lt Lieutenant Rose RAMC No 1 received inspecting probable new quarters in HEIMBACH	
"	-		An N.C.O. & Pte reported to unit as our inspection of the RAMC	
"	-		Army M.O. Room at COLOGNE by H.R.H. The Duke of Connaught	
"	-	9	The unit moved to HEIMBACH - The Herr Schönbeck was taken	
"	-		over for Hospital purposes and for accommodation of personnel	
HEIMBACH	-	10	The C.O. & an N.C.O. attended a Conference at 6th C.C.S. in case the	
"	-		position of War memorial to the R.A.M.C who had fallen during the war	
"	-	12	An RAMC reinforcement arrived	
"	-	13	The CO attended a J.C.M at Ht Fussenich	
"	-	15	The CO attended a Conference at office of ADMS	
"	-	16	20 infantry arrived (to be attached to the unit) for training	
"	-	17	" "	
"	-	19	3 O.R. were reinforcements from the RAMC	

WAR DIARY
or
INTELLIGENCE SUMMARY.

(Erase heading not required.)

Army Form C. 2118.

Instructions regarding War Diaries and Intelligence Summaries are contained in F. S. Regs., Part II. and the Staff Manual respectively. Title pages will be prepared in manuscript.

Place	Date	Hour	Summary of Events and Information	Remarks and references to Appendices
HEIMBACH	1919 May 20		B.O.R. was demolished from the W. Range of the mid-	a/4
	22		24 - B. of Breakey Range was transferred to the 3rd Platoon & Struck off Strength of this unit.	a/4
			The CO attended a Conference at Office of ADMS	a/4
	23		1st Wheeler B.of Warning order to move & munit. to Opladen received	a/4
			2 O.R. was demolished from the W. Range of this unit -	a/4
	26		12 O.R. was transferred to this Unit from 2/2 W.R. Amb & taken on Strength	a/4
			IV Corps Medical arrangements in event of move forward - received	a/4
	27		9 O.R. was demolished from the Range of this unit.	a/4
	29		10 O.R. " " " " " "	a/4

[signatures]

O.C. 2/1ST W.R. FIELD AMBULANCE.

Army Form C. 2118.

WAR DIARY
or
INTELLIGENCE SUMMARY.

(Erase heading not required.)

Instructions regarding War Diaries and Intelligence Summaries are contained in F. S. Regs., Part II. and the Staff Manual respectively. Title pages will be prepared in manuscript.

Place	Date	Hour	Summary of Events and Information	Remarks and references to Appendices

(A9475) Wt W2355/P360 600,000 12/17 D. D. & L. Sch. 82a- Forms/C2118/15.

Army Form C. 2118.

WAR DIARY
or
INTELLIGENCE SUMMARY.

(Erase heading not required.)

Instructions regarding War Diaries and Intelligence Summaries are contained in F. S. Regs., Part II. and the Staff Manual respectively. Title pages will be prepared in manuscript.

Place	Date	Hour	Summary of Events and Information	Remarks and references to Appendices

CONFIDENTIAL

WAR DIARY
of

~~HEADQUARTERS~~
~~G.W. Reinft. R.A.M.C.~~ 3/1st (W.R.) Field Amb.

from 1st July 1919 to 31st July 1919

VOLUME XXXI

Army Form C. 2118.

WAR DIARY
or
INTELLIGENCE SUMMARY.
(Erase heading not required.)

Place	Date	Hour	Summary of Events and Information	Remarks and references to Appendices
DUREN	July 1/19		The unit moves to HEIMBACH — taking up the same billets as previously occupied. One O.R. R.A.M.C. demobilised.	AHS
HEIMBACH	- 2nd		The D.A.D.S. & A.D.M.S. together visited the unit.	AHS
	- 4th		An R.A.S.E. (M.T.) reinforcement arrived	AHS
	- 5th		The A.D.M.S. together with Officers from the Siamese Army visited the unit.	AHS
	- 8th		An R.A.S.E. (M.T.) O.R. was demobilised	AHS
	- 9th		A General Holiday was granted for Peace festivities.	AHS
	- 11th		The D.D.M.S. with A.D.M.S. visited the unit to examine its	AHS
	- 15th		49 Infantry attached to the R.A.M.C. — All were approved for transfer.	AHS
	- 19th		A General Holiday was granted in view of the celebration of Peace throughout the British Empire	AHS

WAR DIARY
INTELLIGENCE SUMMARY

Army Form C. 2118.

Place	Date	Hour	Summary of Events and Information	Remarks and references to Appendices
HEINBACH	July	22nd	Lt.Col. A.G. HEBBLETHWAITE D.S.O. handed over to me and proceeded to U.K. for demobilization	July
		23rd	Authority for transfer of +9 property attg. to this unit, to R.A.v.C. new unit received (allotted)	July
		26	Authority (DMS RHINE ARMY P1184/192 -7-19) for appointment of Capt G.W. REA as Section Commander "B" Sect as from 21-6-19.	July
		29	S.S.M. Kendall, R.A.S.C. H.T. proceeded to Construction Camp Cologne for demobilization	July
		30	The O.R. P.B. man (8th Worcesters) att. R.A.S.C. H.T. proceeded for demobilization	July
		31	Attended conference at 64 CCS Bologne	

Gunter
Major R.A.v.C.

Army Form C2118.

WAR DIARY
or
INTELLIGENCE SUMMARY.

Volume XXXI MEDICAL

(Erase heading not required.)

Confidential
War Diary (Medical)
of
1/1st West Riding Field Ambulance
From 1st Augt 1919 To 31st Augt 1919
VOLUME

WAR DIARY
or
INTELLIGENCE SUMMARY.

(Erase heading not required.)

Army Form C.

Place	Date	Hour	Summary of Events and Information	Remarks and references to Appendices
HEIMBACH Army of Rhine	AUGUST 8.		D.M.S. Rhine Army, D.D.M.S. IV Corps and A.D.M.S. 60th Division nearly the ambulance.	
			700 R.A.S.C. (H.T.) demobilized.	W.K.C.
DUREN	9.	10.30	Unit entrained for DUREN on way to ENGLAND.	W.K.B
		19.00	Unit left DUREN	W.K.B
	10.		In train for CALAIS	W.K.C.
CALAIS	11.	7.00	Arrived CALAIS	W.K.B
		12.30	Embarked on "PRINCE LEOPOLD" for FOLKESTONE.	W.K.B
ENGLAND		14.30	Disembarked at FOLKESTONE.	W.K.B
		19.20	Leave FOLKESTONE for LONDON	W.K.C.
		21.20	Arrive LONDON	W.K.B
		23.00	Leave KINGS CROSS for CATTERICK.	W.K.B
	12.	06.00	Arrived CATTERICK BRIDGE STATION	W.K.B
CATTERICK CAMP		8.20	Leave CATTERICK BRIDGE in Camp Railway for CATTERICK CENTRAL	W.K.B
		8.45	Arrive CATTERICK CENTRAL Station and marched Howitzers since Scotton Camp?	G.P.B
	13	9.00	Parade daily for inspection by commanding officer afterwards physical training, squad drill and R.R	M.R.
	19.	11.00	Route march	W.P.C
			One hours educational training.	L.O.B
	22.		Captain W.K. CHURCHOUSE M.C. R.A.M.C. reports for duty.	
	23-31		MAJOR G.W. REA hands over command of unit to Capt W.K.CHURCHOUSE and proceeds on 15 days furlough	L.O.B
			Daily parades as above	L.O.B
	29.		Sergt PARKES and two men R.A.M.C.T. and one man R.A.M.C. demobilized	L.O.B

W.P.Churchouse
Capt. R.A.M.C.
Ofr i/c 2(L.W.F.) F.A.

www.ingramcontent.com/pod-product-compliance
Lightning Source LLC
Chambersburg PA
CBHW081407160426
43193CB00013B/2127